THE MIND OF WALL STREET

Compliments of

The Mind of
Wall Street

LEON LEVY

WITH EUGENE LINDEN

Foreword by Alan Abelson

PublicAffairs

New York

Book design and composition by Mark McGarry, Texas Type & Book Works
Set in Electra

Library of Congress Cataloging-in-Publication data
Levy, Leon, 1929–2003
The mind of Wall Street / Leon Levy with Eugene Linden ; foreword by
Alan Abelson.— 1st ed.
p. cm.
Includes index.
ISBN 1-58648-208-4 (pbk.)
1. Wall Street. 2. Investments—United States. 3. Speculation—United States.
I. Linden, Eugene. II. Title.
HG4910 .L463 2002
332.6'0973—dc21
2002031856

10 9 8 7 6 5 4 3 2

To my father, Jerome,
and to my brother, Jay,
and my nephew, David,
who have kept the flame
of Dad's economics alive

Contents

Foreword

by Alan Abelson

WALL STREET has a lot to answer for. In the late 1990s, it filled the popular imagination with dreams of avarice and seduced otherwise sane human beings into indulging in a once-in-a-generation orgy of speculation. In the process, it suborned accountants, turned stock analysts into shills, and aided and abetted the machinations of the worst and sleaziest of corporate America. But perhaps the most unforgivable of its many monstrous sins has been to inspire scores of bad books by bored billionaire investors, eager to inflict on the masses every detail of their tinsel triumphs and vapid ruminations.

So far as I can determine, there has been no scientific study of the origin of this extraordinary outbreak of truly terrible books by authors, who, besides an ability to accumulate an enormous amount of money, are distinguished primarily by an inexplicably high regard for themselves. Whatever their virtues—and everybody presumably has some, after all—coherence of thought and clarity of expression are not prominent among them. Not a few, in fact, offer living proof that not only can illiterates function, but they can prosper as well.

In any case, what the world surely doesn't need is another bad book. Especially another bad investment book. There already are more than enough to satisfy even the most masochistic taste, and every day their numbers swell. If this seems a peculiar way to begin an admiring note on *The Mind of Wall Street* and its remarkable author, Leon Levy—well, yes, it certainly is. Yet, not the least of this book's appeal is that it is so strikingly different from the run-of-the-mill efforts dribbled out by the Wall Street illiterati, just as Leon Levy stands out as a man conspicuously apart from the ordinary successful investment professional.

Part financial memoir by an unfailingly curious and uncommonly insightful spectator, part subtle and pragmatic investment guide by a master investor, and part examination of human psychology as one of the dominant movers and shakers of markets, this book is as removed from a dry-as-dust academic treatise as Heaven is from Hades. More than that, it's pure Leon: discursive at times, informed and witty, and absent the slightest trace of condescension. And it is spiced from first to last with a liberal seasoning of anecdote about this tumultuous and extraordinary era's great financial personages and great financial rogues (I run the risk here of being redundant), many of whom Leon observed up close and with not a few of whom he engaged in hand-to-hand combat.

"Transparency" is all the rage these days, so in the interest of full disclosure I might as well 'fess up to some intimate details of my relationship with Leon Levy. Leon and I have known each other since high school and college. The qualities that make Leon such a terrific human being—warmth and generosity, profound intelligence, wonderfully self-deprecating humor, unflagging curiosity about just everything in the wide world, and a way of looking at things from an often revealingly askew perspective—animate his narrative. The boy, I guess, is father to the man, and just about all these qualities were visible when we were in Townsend Harris High School together sixty years ago. Notably among them was a certain abstracted air that Leon refers to in his book as usually taken for "absent-mindedness." He slyly insists he wasn't absent-minded at all, but merely "thinking of other things."

That Leon is a brave fellow is attested to by his choice of a title: *The Mind of Wall Street*. Man, talk about serving up a straight line! Typically Leon, though, is his preemptive riposte to the obvious cracks that would inevitably greet the coupling of mind and Wall Street. He's quick to explain he was uniquely qualified to examine the mind of Wall Street in light of the fact that in college he received an A+ in abnormal psychology.

For both the economy and the stock market, the roughly fifty years that the book spans were epochal in every sense of the word. Their massive embrace, so adroitly and flavorfully described by Leon, took in a fecundity and variety of change that was as bewildering as it was breathtaking. Not the least of the momentous events that were to shape those fifty years occurred early on, when the Depression mentality that had instilled such restraint on both the economy and the stock market finally was dissipated.

The decades that followed were about evenly marked by innovation and excess, explosive growth and corrosive slump. Just as they were in the real world, the 1960s on Wall Street were a hyper time. They started with a speculative frenzy that went bust and they ended with an even more frenetic speculative frenzy that went bust. In many ways, the 1960s were a dress rehearsal for the late 1990s: the celebration of money managers as contemporary heroes, the discovery by the captains of commerce and industry of the uses of accountancy to kit their stock, the lust for acquisitions to create the illusion of growth, the craze for IPOs and all the evils that issued from it, the shuttle of speculative contagion that ran back and forth between Wall Street and corporate America.

The 1970s began as an exacerbation of the 1960s, but more concentrated, and then ended up as their economic and investment polar opposite. The decade featured the devaluation of the dollar and the oil embargo, both of which helped touch off an astonishing commodity inflation that flared for the better part of the decade and manifested itself most amusingly and insanely in the rage for all manner of collectibles, from comic books to gold coins.

The 1980s, for their part, and with the always handy advantage of hindsight, were a mini-preview of the opening years of this new century. Most particularly, the scintillating sight they afforded was of tycoons in handcuffs (the tycoons then happened to be big Wall Street traders and the more recent tycoons happened to be big corporate CEOs—but they're certainly the same under the skin). The decade also was a huge incubator of financial engineering that enhanced humanity with such marvelous artifacts as junk bonds and offered absolute immunity to investors with that ingenious device known as portfolio insurance (see the events of October 19, 1987).

The great bubble mania of the 1990s that infected half the population is still fresh in memory, the debris of its bursting still very much in evidence. The wounds to the economy and to millions of investors are still deep and raw. It was as if the whole country went nuts for four or five years—great fun for a professional spectator like me and perfect material for anyone with an abiding interest in abnormal psychology like Leon.

As all the foregoing suggests, gentle skeptic that he is, a tolerant, amused but sharp and anthropological observer, Leon couldn't have chosen a more fertile fifty years to immerse himself in Wall Street. And the yield from that immersion for the reader of this book is absolutely bountiful. It has, to cite one example among so many, the best, most concise, and clearest explanation for the collapse of Long-Term Capital Management that threatened to unhinge the entire global financial system.

But the real treat for the reader of *The Mind of Wall Street* is to get to know Leon Levy as the amiable, incredibly informed and brilliant soul we who have had the pleasure of his company all these years have the privilege of knowing.

Introduction

═══════

FOR A GOOD PART of my life, I read about the great booms and busts of history—the South Sea bubble, the tulip mania, the 1929 crash—but in the late 1990s, I knew my bubble had finally come.

I've had two loves in my life: One is the stock market, the other psychology. Nothing ever happens without people making decisions. Even the bubbles wouldn't be worth talking about without discussing the psychology that drove them. The moods of the market affect not only stock prices but also the fortunes of business.

The Internet stock craze convinced me that there has never been a more important time to come to grips with what has happened to the markets, what we have brought upon ourselves, and where I think this will lead.

So, in early 2000, as the Nasdaq and the Dow were powering to all-time highs, I decided to write a book about my two great passions.

Two and a half years later, in the summer of 2002, the great financial reckoning that has followed the stock market mania of the 1990s continues to gather momentum. We have been treated to the sight of congressmen who earlier helped weaken the oversight of markets and accounting now rising in high dudgeon against the executives of firms such as Enron, Adelphia, and WorldCom, who took advantage of congressional laxity and investor inattention to line their pockets. We have the spectacle of analysts trying to explain how they could disparage a stock in private e-mails while maintaining the highest buy recommendations in their public statements, even as the companies they recommended hurtled toward bankruptcy. We have seen case after case of companies that used accounting trickery to report strong "pro forma" earnings right up to the point of defaulting on their obligations for lack of cash, and we have seen a parade of accountants who suddenly seem to have found basic accounting very difficult to understand.

The posturing would be entertaining were it not for the $7 trillion or so in value that has been wiped out since the market peak, ruining the dreams and retirement plans of countless Americans. There is more to come. My instincts, refined by fifty years of experience in finance, tell me that we are in but the third act of a five-act Shakespearean drama that portends a bad ending. Stock prices may have plummeted from their dizzying heights, but neither consumers nor investors have yet realized the perils of the suffocating pall of debt hanging over the financial world. Nor have they reckoned with the increasing difficulty of competing in a global market burdened with excess capacity and idled workers in almost every industry. Even at today's discounted prices, the markets have yet to digest that the massive tide of foreign money that flowed into the markets in the past decade is ebbing and may begin to flow out, and consumers have only just begun to save more and spend less (a nearly inevitable result of harder times that will drive the last acts of this drama).

We've been here before, of course. That's the good news. The bad news is that one of those "befores" was the 1930s, when it took more than a decade and a world war to digest the excesses of the 1920s. We've had other booms and busts as well—in the go-go 1960s and in the high-flying 1980s with Ivan Boesky, Michael Milken, and others.

This revisitation points to a larger age-old theme: Good times breed laxity, laxity breeds unreliable numbers, and ultimately, unreliable numbers bring about bad times. This simple rhythm of markets is as predictable as human avarice. Regulatory and accounting laxness is easily ignored when stock prices are climbing, but as companies cut corners and hide expenses (to keep prices rising so that executives can exercise options and get their bonuses), they set up a day of reckoning. At some point, bankers, bondholders, or other investors will demand proof that a company has the money to pay its debts. That is when the party ends and the hangover begins. Markets fall, and exaggerated earnings and reduced oversight become very important indeed.

The cast of bad guys is also familiar. Over time, those with capital get used to the fact that the most aggressive and persuasive people approaching them for financing are not always the most scrupulous. The public now is getting a taste of what financiers have long encountered. In the late 1990s, we witnessed a phenomenon in which the unscrupulous turned to ordinary Americans as a source of capital, taking advantage of the teenage romance between first-time investors and the rising stock market. Fast-talking promoters—as well as respected brokerage firms and mutual funds—spoke of "new paradigms" and the unlimited potential of the Internet, and the public bought it.

No one has the excuse of claiming that there were no omens of impending disaster. *The Wall Street Journal, Barron's,* and *The New York Times* reported ably and responsibly on accounting laxity and the dangers of margin debt. Even as the market became overheated in the late 1990s, the financial press sounded many alarms about the myriad other monsters lurking beneath the waves. But, to borrow a phrase from Bob Dole, where was the outrage? Now that financial shenanigans have cost investors trillions, everybody wants to tighten accounting standards and address other abuses. It has been ever thus. For four hundred years, history shows, governments impose tighter standards only after a market crashes.

An upbeat market leaves the public unmindful of bad news, whereas during a down market, no one trusts good news. Amid the pain of the recession that dogged the first years of the Reagan administration, it was not at all obvious that this downturn represented one of the best buying opportunities for stocks for the balance of the century. Many investors in 1982, embittered by the wallowing stock market of the previous decade, found it psychologically difficult to jump headlong into stocks. Writing in *The New York Times*, Floyd Norris noted that James Freeman, the director of research at First Boston, warned that the market was poised "to take the ultimate dive," precisely as the great bull market of the next two decades began.

Investors were often scared off by experts like Freeman who predicted disaster. In 1982 the United States was suffering through a deep recession, but that year also marked the final taming of the great inflation of the 1970s, which had undermined confidence in the economy and in the dollar for much of that decade. Once the Federal Reserve's restrictions on the money supply broke the back of inflation, interest rates fell. The new Reagan administration also reduced tax rates and regulations that had restrained businesses in the past. If in 1982 an investor had imagined himself in a low-interest, business-friendly environment—rather than a high-interest, regulatory regime—he might have then sensed the coming surge in capital spending that contributed mightily to the growth of earnings and soaring stock prices in the coming years.

However, it was perfectly reasonable, given the psychological mood of the times, for investors to sit on the sidelines. Investors are very good at recognizing the moods of the past—for example, the Roaring Twenties, the Great Depression, the Swinging Sixties—but we tend to be oblivious to the mood of the present. When do we notice that the world has changed?

Sometimes change arrives with a bang. The dropping of the atomic bomb on Hiroshima instantly and permanently changed the stakes of great-power conflicts. But more often, change creeps upon us incrementally, punctuated by upheavals that, often as not, are rationalized as part of business as usual. Only later do we realize that the world has been turned on its head. Few of the press witnessing the first televised presidential debate between John F. Kennedy and Richard Nixon in 1960 realized then that this emerging medium had profoundly altered the way campaigns would be run hence-forth. Indeed, sometimes it is the most trivial events that jog us into noticing grand changes in society.

At the height of the last bull market, I read that the state pension fund in California fired one of its managers because he had invested in U.S. Treasury bonds. Concerned about the overheated market, the manager simply sought to protect his fund against a market decline. His bosses thought he was being foolishly conservative. Certainly, the firing of a fund manager is not the most earthshaking news compared with events such as the 1997 collapse of Thailand's currency, the baht; the Russian default a year later; the accounting scandals of 2001–2002; or other recent events that have sent tremors through the financial world. The item about the unfortunate fund manager caught my attention, however, because five decades earlier, when I arrived on Wall Street, the protocol was precisely the opposite. In most states it was *illegal* for a trust fund manager to invest more than a small percentage of fund assets in stocks. To a fund manager from the 1950s catapulted into the late 1990s, the notion that someone could be fired for investing in bonds would make no sense, somewhat akin to hearing that ice cream was good for you. Back then, with memories of the Great Depression still fresh, those entrusted with other people's money eschewed stocks as too risky.

Thus, this little item in the paper served as a tap on the shoulder, reminding me about the extraordinary times of the late 1990s. What does it mean that in the space of my career on Wall Street, attitudes toward risk could completely reverse? Until the collapse of the Nasdaq, some argued it meant that the world had changed, that we had entered a "new economy" in which new technologies, free-market trade policies, and sophisticated ways of monitoring consumer demand and inventories had made recessions a thing of the past and eliminated the risk in stocks. That was before inventories and industrial capacity ballooned (particularly in "new economy" companies), and the United States entered a recession in 2002.

One can only hope that with experience will come the ability to recognize those things that do not change, even as fashions come and go. I'm fond of the remark, attributed to Mark Twain, that "history does not repeat itself, at best it sometimes rhymes." Over time, I've noticed that investors tend to invoke "new economies" when they want to justify actions that are unjustifiable by conventional analysis. Rather than heralding a new era, the shift in attitudes toward risk exposed a neglected but hugely important attribute of all markets, past, present and future: namely, the role of psychology.

In the 1950s, investors were very much aware that stocks could go down as well as up. It seemed preposterous in the recent heyday of Internet stocks, when earnings were scorned as a drag on growth, but in the 1950s, investors bought stocks when companies earned money. And they sold stocks if they could get a higher return from triple-A high-grade bonds. Investors reasoned that stocks were inherently more risky than bonds, and thus when dividend yields dropped below bond yields, stocks were overpriced. Imagine the scorn that would have greeted the investor who attempted to apply that rule in 1999. He would have ended up with a portfolio of cigarette companies, perhaps a utility, and little else. Three years later, however, a company's earnings are once again attracting attention.

Until the Internet bubble popped in 2000 and the broader markets began to fall as well, most investors—anyone born after 1960—had experienced only the great bull market that began in 1982. With the exception of the brief but terrifying crash of 1987 and a short recession in 1991, the lesson for investors up to 2000 was that stocks ultimately rise. Consequently, it's not at all surprising that investors were willing to believe theories of the market that would have been viewed as ludicrous if presented a few decades earlier.

To find the last time investors were that ebullient, we must go back to just before the crash of 1929. Then, financial journals were filled with eerily similar arguments that a new economy was dawning that would cause stock prices to rise for the foreseeable future. Given the enormous impact of the cheap automobile, mass production manufacturing, and the proliferation of radio, the telephone, and electrification, it is arguable that the 1920s had a better claim on the concept of a new economy than did the technophiles of seven decades later. (Indeed, the development of mass production techniques in the 1920s later made possible the U.S. mobilization in World War II.) No matter, "old economy" realities exposed the vulnerabilities of that "new economy" as well.

This pattern of generational forgetting may be obvious and simple, but it has profound effects. Markets affect investor psychology, but investor psychology also affects markets. Basically, we all live three lives: our life, the life of our parents, and that of our children. Events within our experience, particularly our youth, remain the most visceral in memory, but events that lie beyond the horizon of these generations tend to be more abstract, if only because they don't have an immediate connection to our lives. I might warn a Young Turk incessantly about the horrors of a crash or bad market, but I will not likely make an impression on one who hasn't lived through the experience. If societies can forget and then repeat the horrors of war, they can certainly forget the temporary ruination of a stock market crash.

Try to imagine the role of psychology in your investing. What were you thinking or feeling when you bought or sold a stock or bond? What prompted you to pick up the telephone? To what degree did mood and intuition, as opposed to analysis, affect the decision? What assumptions caused you to pay heed to a particular piece of information? Why did you weigh one piece of information over another? What facts did you include in your decision?

Then try to imagine what the person on the other side of the trade was thinking. Investors tend to forget that whoever buys the stock you sell or sells the stock you buy has undertaken his own analysis of the situation. There is a genius on one side of every trade and a dolt on the other, but which is which does not become clear until much later.

Investing is as much a psychological as an economic act. Even hardheaded types who think they are basing their decisions on fundamentals will discover over time that there are fashions in fundamentals. This, in turn, suggests that fundamentals are sometimes not so fundamental after all. In the 1970s, many investors waited each Thursday afternoon for the Federal Reserve to release the figures for M1, an indicator of the money supply, whereupon they might buy or sell depending on whether M1 was exceeding or failing to meet expectations. The crowd that waits for news of changes in M1 before making investment decisions has all but disappeared.

Despite all the evidence that markets float atop an ocean of beliefs and moods, conventional economics minimizes the role of psychology in freely functioning markets. This is odd, since both market seers and economists talk endlessly about the mood of markets. When they sit down to analyze a stock, sector, or market, however, they tend to look upon markets as rational and efficient.

This outlook is very dangerous for one's economic health. It's even more dangerous to misconstrue success in the markets for rational analysis. Those most adept at profiting from a particular market are often least likely to notice when the game is over, and probably the least psychologically prepared to profit from the successor market. Why should they change something that has worked so well for them? Most of the heroes of the "go go" years in the 1960s turned out to be goats in the 1970s. How the heroes of the great bull market of the late 1990s will fare in the years to come remains to be seen.

But the market has even crueler twists. It's not sufficient that a player figure out when the game has changed. When a market shifts, it usually requires the investor to adopt a psychological stance anathema to the precepts upon which he built his earlier success. It will not be easy for the apostles of the so-called new economy to nimbly adjust should the market decide that quaint old-economy obsessions such as earnings and dividends are important after all.

The message is that mood or investor psychology is as important to markets as is information. It requires tremendous discipline to apply this understanding to one's behavior. I encountered a particularly vivid example of this paradox in 1962. At the time, President Kennedy was jawboning the steel industry not to raise prices, and I believed we were about to enter a recession. My colleagues and I at Oppenheimer and Company brought together our top money managers and asked them for their take on the prospects for the market in general and the particular stocks they followed. All agreed with me that the market was likely to decline. Then I looked at how they rated the expected performance of their particular stocks. I added these estimates and averaged them, to find that these same managers were predicting that their stocks would rise collectively by 15 percent. In fact, our fund fell about 30 percent.

For most people, the most dangerous self-delusion is that even a falling market will not affect their stocks, which they bought out of a canny understanding of value. Piling delusion upon delusion, most people also believe that no matter what happens, they will be able to get out at or near the top of the market.

Both ideas are dead wrong. Demonstrating the latter is a matter of simple arithmetic. Most investors who sell shares are switching their investments from one stock to another. Only a small percentage are switching from stocks to bonds or cash. Let's say that each year, turnover is 70 percent of all shares listed on all the exchanges. And let's say that 10 percent of all stocks sold in a year are by people leaving the market. That means only 7 out of every 100 shares are being sold by people who want cash instead of stock. The odds of cashing out at the top the year the market peaks are thus 7 out of 100 or about 1 in 15. Only a few investors will get out there. The rest will be stuck, either waiting for the price to return to its heights (many people retain the belief that the market somehow knows or cares what price they paid for a stock), or settling for lesser gains or losses.

When a stock plummets, money vanishes. The $400 billion in market value of Cisco that disappeared during the Nasdaq swoon and the $70 billion decline in Enron market value represent money that has disappeared, except for the tiny fraction of that amount that went into the pockets of those who sold as the stock plummeted. The market capitalization that vanished has real effects: There is that much less money to finance investment or consumption.

Lost along with this money is the crucial element of trust. The lesson for the public has been that neither companies nor the analysts supposedly assessing those companies' prospects can be trusted. Nor can people always trust the independent accountants who certify company reports. They cannot even always trust the financial cops of the Securities and Exchange Commission (SEC) to catch cheaters in a timely fashion. When people don't trust the information or institutions of a market, they won't buy its products.

The market meltdown was a reminder to all of us that no one has a system to beat the market. This is not to say that no one can beat the market, but an investor should greet any promise of automatic returns with great skepticism. Most investors know this, but still, people love systems. I remember once visiting Monte Carlo, where I looked up a friend of my mother's who loved to gamble. She was the widow of a successful accountant, and she kept her husband's ashes in a vase on the mantelpiece, along with the ashes of her favorite dog, Gilligan. One day, watching her play roulette and feeling a little mischievous, I said, "Have you ever noticed that the numbers that come up at the other roulette table often come up at this table a few minutes later?" Without missing a beat, she replied, "Oh, yes, that's the echo effect. A lot of players use it."

The example is absurd, of course, but a similar hunger for order in a capricious world causes even very sophisticated investors to impute their success to equally implausible systems. I've always been suspicious of theories about the nature of markets, and my experience as an investor has only served to harden this bias. It is highly unlikely that any of us will encounter a unified theory of markets—some equation with variables into which an investor can plug numbers and derive an answer as to where to invest. To the degree that markets are governed by psychology, they resist reduction to some neat theory or system.

Apart from the unfathomable aspects of human psychology, there is never perfect knowledge about the world. Simply put, we don't know what we don't know. In the early 1970s, all the calculations for the cost of the Alaska pipeline were thrown out of whack when environmentalists sought injunctions to halt the project until the pipeline's effects on caribou could be studied and addressed. It was thought that the pipeline as then designed would disrupt the normal migratory patterns of the caribou, which survive by eating lichens in one of the most inhospitable climates on earth. Dealing with the caribou delayed the pipeline for about eight years, and since time is money, the changed timetable forced the pipeline's owner, Atlantic Richfield, to reprice the bonds that would finance the project. Caribou, or their equivalents, always have a way of turning up in big projects, and ever since then, investment professionals have referred to such unknowns as "the caribou factor."

If human nature makes markets inefficient and moody, and the caribou factor defeats the most exquisite analysis of financiers, it is natural to ask how anyone might hope to make money in the markets. Markets may be inherently unpredictable—the efficient-market theorists are right about that—but there are always clues in the actions of government and in the behavior of major economic actors that offer guidance for the attentive about developments that offer opportunities.

A good idea, a long-term perspective, and the creativity to implement a strategy to profit from your insight are necessary to prosper in finance, but they are not sufficient. None of these qualities will bear fruit unless you have the discipline to stay with your strategy when the market tests your confidence, as it inevitably will. When you have made a massive bet and markets start to go against you, it is always a good idea to reexamine the assumptions behind your strategy. Even if you are still convinced you are right, however, it is difficult to resist the temptation to cut losses or take a quick profit.

In such circumstances, it is easy to lose sight of the fact that ultimately the market does reflect value, even if it may seem to lose its marbles for unbearably long periods. Investors must decide how long they are willing to wait. Investors also have to be alert to changes in the market that could change their original assumptions. We may not have an efficient market, but we do have a pretty efficient market. Or as the legendary value investor Benjamin Graham once put it: In the short term, the market is like a voting machine, reflecting a company's popularity, but over the long term, it more resembles a weighing machine, reflecting a company's true value. This is the aspect of markets that allows the great investors to outdistance those who are lucky.

Now we are learning that the great bull market of the past decade was built almost entirely on illusions. The new economy was slain by old-economy realities. Much of the earnings growth was the result of bookkeeping sleight-of-hand. Even the notion that stocks always outperform bonds over the long run—the mantra that lured so many first-timers into the market—is now under attack as various economists argue that the numbers are far more even when adjusted for stocks that have disappeared from the market, and discounted for the risk inherent in the volatility of stock prices.

Why should the market be any more perfect than the very human emotions and calculations that drive it? Investors overreact, and so do markets. Investors get swept up in moods, and so do markets. And this interplay creates investment opportunities.

1

Reason Does Not Prevail

WHEN I WAS A YOUNG MAN growing up in New York City, I could never imagine that anyone would pay me to do anything. I did not do particularly well in school, I am easily distracted, and I have always been forgetful—not the list of personality traits likely to appear in a help-wanted ad for any profession. Still, from the age of thirteen, when I invested in the stock market $200 that I had received as bar mitzvah presents, I always believed I could make money with money. This turned out to be true. In fact, had my father allowed me to buy American Cities Power & Light Class B at 2 cents a share, I would have become rich at a very young age, as the stock rose to over $3 a share.

I joined the newly formed investment firm Oppenheimer and Co. in 1951 as one of its first partners, and I have never really had another job. I played a role in the building of the firm, I founded the Oppenheimer Fund (which subsequently had many offspring), and along the way I participated in some of the events that helped transform the investment world from a clubby, inbred, and self-perpetuating community into the massive, hydra-headed industry we have today.

These innovations and events might seem unconnected, even random. They also include taking a company out of bankruptcy in a way that dramatically illustrated the opportunities for profit in distressed companies, and using leveraged buyouts as a way of unlocking the hidden value of companies during an era of depressed securities prices.

Apart from being immensely profitable, all these events had one other common element: They represented unexploited financial opportunities. Many of the innovations my colleagues and I pioneered are now familiar, but when we began, they were unknown, ignored, or unloved. Certainly, I've had many ideas that did not turn out well, but in the course of my investing career, I've been able to prosper despite the fact that the economy and markets have changed enormously.

I'm sure these accomplishments baffle anyone who meets me for the first time. I can even sense the question forming in the person's mind: "How does a guy who can't find his pipe when smoke is coming out of his pocket manage to do so well?" After talking to me a while, I'm sure people are even more mystified and leave the conversation convinced that it must be luck, that the heavy lifting has been done by my partners, or that I'm due for a fall.

To a degree, all of these things are true. I'm certain that much of what passes for successful investing on Wall Street has to do with luck or coincidence, and certainly, I've had my share of good fortune. On the other hand, I've had bad luck, too.

I never wanted to do anything alone; I have always liked having bright people around me, and I often get new ideas from talking with people. So I always had partners—and of course this meant that sometimes they didn't agree with me, and sometimes they were right. I was fortunate, early on, in meeting Jack Nash, who has a great gift for running an organization and superb instincts for seeing trouble ahead. He was my partner for almost fifty years.

Unlike most people on Wall Street, I never went to business school, and I didn't study business in college. (I majored in psychology at the City College of New York and was turned down when I attempted to get into the course on advanced securities analysis.) I grew up with a father who believed that economics was the discipline that could lead to greater social equity, and in our household, the dynamics of business were discussed as routinely as other families discussed the daily news. My father wanted to solve the problems of unemployment and to see a fairer distribution of wealth. He devoted his life to the study of economics.

As a teenager, what I knew about business came through reading tales of the robber barons of the nineteenth century. I remember vividly the story of how Jay Gould, who controlled the Erie Railroad, outmaneuvered his archrival, Cornelius Vanderbilt, who ran the New York Central Railroad. Both wanted to lock up the lucrative business of shipping cattle from Chicago to New York, and so they got into a price war. As they undercut each other, the price for shipping a carload of cattle from Chicago to New York dropped to a fraction of what would sustain a profit. Then Gould changed tactics. He bought up every steer in Chicago, raised the price of shipping by the Erie road to full price, and shipped his cattle to New York on the New York Central, thereby getting Vanderbilt to subsidize his cattle venture.

This saga was more colorful than today's studies of pricing anomalies in the derivatives market. Unencumbered by the received wisdom of a business education, I had to figure things out for myself. If you think things through for yourself, you may waste some time, but you also may stumble onto something that has been ignored or disregarded. Doing so has enabled me to look at the financial world with fresh eyes.

I know that to many people, especially my wife, Shelby—whom I once left stranded at a party because I forgot she had come with me—I appear absent-minded and distracted. But usually, I'm simply thinking about something else. This trait, however, has proved very useful on Wall Street, where it is all too easy to become swept up in the mood of the times. Quite often when I seem off in the clouds, I'm imagining myself in another time, reacting to events of another time or era, whether those events involve the advent of a common currency for Europe, the crash of 1987, the Internet bubble, or whatever the compelling news of the day might have been—or something totally unrelated.

Indeed, one of the virtues of envisioning the present from a different time is that it underscores the important role of the intangibles, such as mood and psychology, that govern the way we perceive and interpret the supposedly hard numbers upon which investors base their decisions. My attempt to imagine the present as it would look from a different time helps me to sort the real from the illusions that blind us to what is before our eyes.

At the height of the stock market bubble of the 1990s, I played a game with the directors of the Oppenheimer Funds, of which I am chairman. I would ask them to project themselves a few years forward after the markets had crashed, and to put themselves into the mind of a congressional staffer who was charged with orchestrating hearings for the Senate Finance Committee on the causes of the crash of the markets. They thought I was an old fool and paid little attention to me.

Since the collapse of Enron at the end of 2001, much of what I imagined has become real, as Congress has rushed to examine a cri-

sis its members had earlier helped to create. One item on my hypothetical agenda that has since attracted congressional attention is the
role of Wall Street research in the mass stock market hysteria of the
end of the past decade. In a similar vein, various inquisitors now
want to discuss why accounting standards were relaxed in so many
ways—such as permitting companies to hide the costs of takeovers
and options, to lump capital gains from investments with earnings
from operations, to book barter transactions as revenues, and to artfully conceal expenses. (The answer, of course, is that Congress
itself weakened various accounting standards during several
"reforms" in the 1990s.) Accounting is supposed to provide the reality behind the corporate spin. What does it mean if this "reality" is
nothing more than another layer of spin? As we have seen, one result
has been a massive rupture of trust.

If Congress continues to follow my imaginary script, it will eventually get around to asking why the Glass-Steagall Act of 1933 was
repealed in 1999, allowing banks to underwrite and sell stocks. Glass-
Steagall had outlawed this egregious conflict of interest—banks selling their customers stocks that the banks themselves were
underwriting—that had contributed to the crash of 1929. This practice is legal once again—and a dangerous temptation. Think of it: A
bank is nervous about the $100 million it loaned to windmill.com. If
it underwrites an IPO (initial public offering) for the dotcom, it gets
its loan back, plus a fee for the underwriting, and if the bank's customers buy the stock, it also gets a commission. Very tempting
indeed. Still, I doubt we will see Congress reviewing the repeal of
Glass-Steagall, since it was by Congress's own action (with Alan
Greenspan's enthusiastic endorsement) that the law was repealed.

At the time when I was imagining the postcrash investigations,
the markets were at their giddiest, and most pundits were dreaming
up reasons why this euphoria could go on forever. My fantasy Senate

hearing served as a way in which I could understand the absurdity of the mania even as it was running rampant. Imagining the aftermath of the bubble helped me understand the bubble itself.

I had proposed this imaginary hearing to my fellow board members as a way of getting them also to think about the perils of the market in the late 1990s. As the decade progressed, and stock prices soared to unprecedented levels, it became clear to me that the U.S. stock exchanges began exhibiting more and more telltale symptoms of a market in the grip of a speculative mania. At one point, the market value of Priceline.com, which encouraged consumers "to name your own price for airline tickets," exceeded that of the major airlines combined. By 2001, it would be worth one one-hundredth of its peak valuation.

Even established companies in the so-called new economy traded at prices that assumed the companies would enjoy unprecedented growth in profits and sales many years into the future. The markets ignored bad news while stocks rocketed on press releases and rumors. Emboldened by the "wealth effect," a temporary insanity brought on by the promise of profits and soaring real estate prices, debt-saddled Americans continued to spend. I had seen euphoric markets before, but never one like this.

In the half century since I began working on Wall Street, there have been several previous turning points, and each has brought low former masters of the universe. Some shifts have been obvious, as when the optimism of the 1960s gave way to uncertainty and pessimism brought about by the Vietnam War and then the Arab oil embargo in 1973. More often, however, the changes have been subtle.

No bell rings when the market changes its emphasis. The market integrates several different time scales into a cacophony—or a symphony, depending on the temperament of the listener. Prices respond to the news of the day, to technical factors pertaining to particular stocks; they respond to political events here and abroad; they respond to market players trying to guess how people will react to events; they respond to technological change and shifts in trade policies; they respond to long-term phenomena, such as the aging of baby boomers and trends in capital spending. At one moment, the mood in one aspect of the market may be ebullient, while elsewhere it is morose; the entire market gets swept along by a tide of emotion. Intellectual measures often seem not to apply.

But when has reason ever prevailed in markets? Only in the eye of the beholder, when the market agrees with his analysis. Yes, there are periods when prices seem to closely track world events, but the timing of when prices respond to events can be profoundly affected by psychology. In the markets, timing can be the difference between a windfall and bankruptcy. As the great British economist and philosopher John Maynard Keynes noted, markets can remain irrational longer than you can remain solvent.

To ignore the psychological component of the flux of the markets is to miss seeing the elephant in the room. I would not bet heavily on the longevity of someone who walks into a room with his eyes closed when an elephant is in there, too. Psychology plays a role in all the events of the market, from the actions of the day trader riding the momentum of Internet stocks to the broad long-term shifts that become obvious and undeniable only over time.

Ignoring the maelstrom of the media—perhaps nothing is more preposterous than the explanations commentators give for price movements on Wall Street on any given day—makes it easier to focus on what is important. It also helps to have a broader perspective. Indeed, I think that one of the greatest mistakes of economics was to separate itself from other disciplines. You can't understand economics without understanding philosophy and history. John Maynard Keynes was the greatest economist of the last century, and he was primarily a philosopher; so was Adam Smith, the greatest economist of the eighteenth century. If intelligence is the ability to integrate, creativity is the ability to integrate information from seemingly unconnected sources, and a measure of both abilities is necessary for long-term success in the markets.

My understanding of markets comes from a wide variety of sources. Perhaps the most important has been a theory about the role of profits in the economy, which I learned at my father's knee. Dad developed theories about what drives economies that have guided my investing throughout my career.

My passion for ancient history and archaeology also gives me perspective. I was brought up in the shadow of Victorian times, and as an adolescent I devoured ancient histories, not the least because they were the raciest stories I could find. Archaeology appealed to me because it deals with the complex and obscure problem of reconstructing the past, often from the most tenuous pieces of evidence. Moreover, archaeology occasionally offers the delicious thrill of finding something that confounds conventional wisdom.

This was the case in Ashkelon, Israel, an excavation that I have sponsored since its launch over twenty years ago. In 1995 the team of Israeli and American researchers uncovered what appeared to be a Roman arch—not surprising, perhaps, since Rome once dominated the region. But this arch had been built more than a thousand years before the rise of Rome. It had been constructed by the much-maligned Philistines, a civilization that, in one of history's ironies, turns out to be at least as sophisticated as the Israelite culture that supplanted it. As Tolstoy once noted, the victors write the histories, but the histories are not always accurate.

My interests in the ancient world have given me insights into the modern world. Investigations into antiquity reveal the extraordinary degree to which politicians and financiers are repeatedly able to fleece civilians when things go wrong. In the early days of the Roman Empire, a shrewd manipulator named Crassus became the richest man in Rome by buying up the rights to collect taxes from citizens beyond the reach of official collectors. Such "tax farming" was initially quite lucrative, as these entrepreneurs discovered they could pocket the difference between the amount collected and the amount they had agreed to pay the emperor. As more and more Romans tried to get in on the act, however, prices of these collection contracts rose to the point that the tax farmers could never collect enough to cover their obligations to Rome. Crassus then called upon his lobbying skills to convince the government to organize one of history's first bailouts. The notion that a financial institution is "too big to fail" has deep roots in history.

One truth of archaeology in particular bears directly on my thinking. Archaeologists have their specialties, and one of the curiosities of the field is that those who specialize in one aspect of antiquity tend to be blind to anything else. Archaeologists who look for pottery sherds will not see coins, and, conversely, those who look for coins will not find sherds. Same dig, but those sifting the soils see entirely different things. So it is with markets.

Most people believe that markets are driven primarily by economic factors, and that psychology plays a minor role. I take the position that markets are driven by both psychological and economic factors. I owe a great debt to economists for their inability to acknowledge the degree to which psychology moves markets. (In this sense, it's unfortunate that economics now seems to be embracing psychology. I suspect that economists will always retain the illusion that numbers can capture mood.) My approach to the markets has been to take a long-term perspective, a natural predilection that has on numerous occasions saved me from getting lost in the froth of daily events. I admit that there is something self-serving in this strategy as well. Long-term goals postpone days of reckoning, and if you can identify a goal that takes a lifetime to achieve, you won't be disappointed.

Today, the unprecedented euphoria that gripped the markets in the 1990s is all but gone. Since the average American has roughly 40 percent of his or her financial assets invested in stocks, where the markets go from here will have great impact on the health of the economy and the mood of the public. We now face a bear market equal in scale and intensity to the bull market that has come to an end. If stock prices can be too high for ten years, they can also be too low for the next decade.

Apart from my long time on Wall Street, I might have one particular advantage in addressing these issues. Even though I have been in the thick of many deals and seismic events on Wall Street, I have always been something of an outsider. In the 1960s, when Oppenheimer was growing rapidly, one of our analysts described me as the partner in charge of interplanetary affairs. I think that was meant as a compliment. And at City College, the only course in which I ever got an A+ was abnormal psychology. What better preparation could there be to tackle the role of psychology in markets?

2

Jerome's Legacy

MUCH OF WHAT I KNOW about investing I learned from my father, Jerome Levy. Dad had his own views of analyzing the economy. Though he was a staunch capitalist, he disapproved of the excesses of Wall Street because he thought that the rewards reaped by the players who ran the game were undeserved since they were disproportionate to the risks they took and disproportionate to their contribution to society. (He would have been apoplectic over executives' gargantuan pay of recent years.) Nevertheless, he spent an awful lot of energy devising his own strategy of investing. Indeed, for a man who did not want his son to go to Wall Street, he was inordinately involved in encouraging me to learn how to value companies as businesses and investments.

Dad's influence looms large over my entire family. I founded the Levy Economics Institute of Bard College in part to carry forward his interest in the social impact of economic policies; my brother Jay became an economist and bases his analysis of the prospects of the economy on ideas Dad developed; and Jay's son, David, carries on this work at the Levy Forecasting Center in Mount Kisco, New York. It's not unusual in America for children to carry on a family business, but in our case, subsequent generations of Levys continue to develop one man's ideas.

Jerome Levy was born in Honesdale, Pennsylvania, in 1882. His father had emigrated from Poland to the United States in 1865. After happily forswearing allegiance to Czar Alexander II, my grandfather became a peddler selling supplies to canal boats working the Delaware & Hudson Canal, a business that collapsed with the new competition from the Erie Railroad. In 1891 my grandfather and his six children moved to Division Street on New York's Lower East Side, where he and a partner started a wholesale dry goods business called Levy and Kadane. This business marriage did not last, and in due course my grandfather went it alone, forming the company of S. J. Levy & Sons.

As the eldest of four sons, Dad fell into the role of protector of his siblings. He was a very tough man, with scars from various fights. He tried boxing as a bantamweight and became sufficiently skilled that several people he fought asked him to manage their boxing careers. As a defense against the Irish gangs that regularly beat up his younger brothers, he formed his own gang called the "Never Sweats." Years later, he and my mother were walking down Madison Avenue when they were greeted by a courtly Irish judge dressed in a bowler hat and Chesterfield. Bowing deeply to my mother, he said, "Madam, your husband had the meanest right hook on Division Street."

Dad was a very proud man, and not one to take lightly any perceived slight of his skills. Admitted to City College in 1897, he tried out for the football team, only to be rejected as too short. Dad promptly formed his own team, composed largely of other varsity rejects, and then challenged the City College team to a game in

Central Park. The Never Sweats (Dad stayed with a name if he liked it) won handily.

Dad was tough because he had to be, but his real interests were intellectual. He took every advanced math course available at City College before he graduated in 1901. Like many young men of his day, he spent a year teaching while he decided what he wanted to do. Typically, he managed to turn this higher calling into a combat sport. It was not his fault. He was assigned to teach school in Hell's Kitchen, then home to some of New York's toughest Irish gangs. Moreover, he taught ungraded night classes, which then served chiefly to provide heated rooms for boys who worked during the day and had little interest in academics. When the principal introduced him to his class, he simply said, "Boys, this is your new teacher." Later he told my father, "If I told them your name was Levy, they would kill you."

As soon as the principal left the room, pandemonium broke out. Attempting to restore order, Dad singled out the largest and most truculent boy and told him to sit down. The boy sneered and said, "Who's going to make me?" or some more colorful version of the same sentiment. Dad decked the young tough with one punch, and the boy hit his head as he fell. The sight of their leader bleeding impressed the class sufficiently that everyone quieted down.

Dad had other challenges from his students, and one encounter started a cascade of events that caught the notice of *The New York Times*. Some days after Dad thrashed another student who had disrupted a fire drill, he boarded a trolley car, which was bombarded by rocks as soon as the doors closed. The *Times* carried an item about this puzzling incident in which a trolley car unaccountably lost all its windows in a coordinated assault. Whatever really happened, this was the family lore by the time I was old enough to hear it.

Abandoning teaching for the more tranquil waters of business, Dad took over his father's company, a wholesale hosiery business, but devoted much of his free time to learning about economics and coming up with inventions, such as a self-supporting stocking for women, which he called "suspension bridge stockings" (they never caught on). He was, in essence, a nineteenth-century man—a great believer in rationality, with a Victorian confidence that the application of reason could solve all problems. This confidence, and his nineteenth-century philosophical bias, were evident in the title he chose for his book about the role of economics in the life of a society. With typical assertiveness, he called his book *Economics Is an Exact Science*. (It's not, of course, as physicists love to point out.)

Dad had begun pondering the basic problems of economics in 1912, after hearing a speech by President William Howard Taft at Cooper Union. Following the speech, a member of the audience asked, "President Taft, what do you tell the man who is a skilled mechanic, has a wife and three children, and can't get a job?" Taft responded, "God knows, I don't."

Taft may have dismissed the matter, but the question lodged in Dad's mind. What would cause a man to hire another man? he wondered. The simple answer was that businessmen hired employees if it would increase their profits. He then asked, Where do profits come from? Drawing on his interest in math, he derived some equations that measured various sources of profits. Capital spending figured largely, but not exclusively, in this analysis. Consumer credit and government deficits figured in as well. The accumulation of inventories produced profits—up to a point—and so did a favorable balance of trade. All these economic activities brought more money into the economy without a compensatory increase in goods; therefore, there was more money competing for the same amount of goods, and that money appeared as profits. Dad knew that in bad times, when businessmen worked extremely hard to make ends meet, profits were low, whereas in boom conditions, businessmen perhaps worked less, but their profits soared. In other words, the entrepreneur's efforts were only one ingredient that went into profits.

Dad's ability to predict the direction of corporate profits led him to astute investing decisions over the years. When the United States entered World War I, the stock market shut down for a while, because everyone thought business would be terrible. By contrast, Dad thought the stimulus from deficit spending to pay for the war would be great for the economy, and he accumulated a relatively large inventory. He was right. Then in the postwar boom, dry goods salesmen offered Dad access to goods in a tight market because he had been buying earlier when no one else would. By this time, however, Dad feared a recession looming as inventories built to speculative levels, and he said, "I'm not buying anything!"

Dad, however, was far more interested in unifying economic, political, and social policy than he was in making money. Motivated by the terrible suffering brought on by the Depression and the lack of an adequate safety net, Dad worried about the inability of a healthy man to find a job. It was essentially a nineteenth-century question—and it is more important than any economic issue we face today. My father thought government should be involved. He was a capitalist, but not a laissez-faire capitalist. He believed his profits equation was a nice forecasting tool, but profits were but one part of the system he wanted to describe. After the war, he spent over a decade trying to describe the proper role of eight other elements, including the working, investing, and money-lending classes, the monetary system, taxation, government, consumers, and land. Later he added another element: self-interest in the sense that each worker experiences the direct benefits of his own work. First he tried to describe the functions and obligations of each element, and then what measures might be taken to make these various functions and obligations work together properly.

Influenced by the British thinker Henry George, among others, Dad played with the idea that the government should own all land and natural resources, and lease the land to those willing to take risks. He believed that no one should be able to profit without taking risks, and he was offended by the image of oil barons lazily reaping millions simply because they chanced to own the land while wild-catters assumed all the risks of drilling for oil. His distaste for Wall Street also derived from his distaste for what he saw as an inherent conflict of interest in the dual role of investment bankers, who sup-posedly served the interests both of companies issuing stock and the customers who bought the securities. Neither he nor I, for that mat-ter, ever met anyone who thought that caught between the interests of the two groups, investment bankers would lean over backward to help the customers.

In economics Dad was ahead of his time, but his attitudes toward women were more suited to the nineteenth century. He was against the Nineteenth Amendment, which gave women the vote. He rea-soned that it would double the number of voters without improving the quality of elections. When Warren G. Harding, one of America's least distinguished presidents, was elected in 1920 in the first national contest after the ratification of the amendment, Dad took this as a complete vindication of his views. He talked about it for years afterward.

Even Dad's religious preferences had a nineteenth-century fla-vor. Although he was Jewish, he was not religious. Philosophically he was inclined toward deism, which did not rule out the existence of God but also did not demand that people picture the deity as an omnipotent figure somewhere up in the sky who spent His time keeping tabs on individual actions.

In 1921, after a short courtship, Dad married Sadie Samuelson. Mother's personality differed starkly in every way. Characteristic of Dad's approach to a problem was his reaction when, in 1929, his banker at the National City Bank asked him to buy the bank's stock at several hundred dollars a share (the bank was trying to raise money to expand the trust department). Noting that this amount represented a vast multiple of the bank's earnings, Dad exploded, "You must be either fools or knaves." He was later proved right when the stock crashed, and, indeed, as late as the 1940s, bank employees were still paying off loans they had taken out to buy the stock. Whereas Dad could be tactless, Mother was socially poised and gracious. Dad was driven by ideas; Mother was not very intellectual, but she was a great bridge player.

By the time I arrived on the scene in 1925, Dad was already somewhat removed from business and devoting an increasing portion of his time to learning about economics. Dad's economic forecast saw a depression looming on the horizon. He was bright enough to see that as a dry goods wholesaler, he was at the mercy of both manufacturers and retailers. With more and more competitors further squeezing profit margins, the choice was either to buy a mill down south and produce his own goods or to liquidate the business. He chose the latter, and, in timely fashion, he sold off the assets just before the crash of 1929.

Dad was never shy about putting his money where his mouth was, and his growing interest in economics also saved him from losing much on his investments during the crash. In the late 1920s, one could see the capital spending boom by simply looking out the window at all the buildings going up, including the Empire State Building. But by 1929 this capital spending boom was winding down (in fact, the developers of the Empire State Building ultimately had to reach as far afield as the farmers in Kansas to find the money to finish this beautiful white elephant). Worried about the buildup in inventories and the decline in capital spending, Dad got out of the market.

Dad knew that capital goods expenditures led to profits for the economy as a whole. He also believed that capital spending rose and fell in long cycles, and that the fading cycle of capital spending foretold weaker profits for companies in the years to come. Scholars still argue about the causes of the Great Depression, but few would argue that the prosperity of the 1920s could have continued if capital spending declined.

Therein lies one of the remarkable similarities between the 1920s and the 1990s: Then, as now, capital spending fueled profits and growth, and then, as now, investors and companies took on more and more debt, believing that this growth would continue forever because the fundamental rules had changed. Now, as then, the capital spending boom inevitably ran its course, exposing the hollowness of any thoughts that we had entered a "new economy."

Dad's fears about the future of the market precipitated a memorable scene with my mother. We were distantly connected to the Loew family of theater chain fame, and amid the turmoil after the crash, Mother ran into some members of the family at a bon voyage party. She asked one of her cousins if the Loews were selling any of their holdings. Told no, she promptly bought some shares. Dad was furious when he found out, because he thought the market was very dangerous at the time. But Mother had the last word—the stock soared following her purchase, before she could even pay for the shares.

I was only four at the time of the crash, but thanks to Dad's good timing, we lived through the 1930s rather comfortably, though Dad did get burned shorting the market during a rally in 1931. This is not to say that we lived rich—Dad hated ostentation and had no great hunger to make money. Investing was in part an intellectual exercise for him, and he gave a good deal of his profit away at the end of the year. Some of his earnings went to sponsor the emigration of families from Germany, as Hitler made life for Jews there intolerable.

The two poles of life in the Levy household on West End Avenue in my childhood were investments and economics. Dad tested his ideas on his children and our friends at dinner. My brother Jay, three years older than I, became an acolyte of Dad's ideas in economics, and I his apprentice in investing. Dad's acumen in investing was really my inheritance, but this does not mean he bequeathed me some formula that I have slavishly applied ever since. From my earliest days, I never believed, as Dad did, that the market was a game rigged by "the boys." (Thirty years after he died, however, it turned out that he may have been right, when it was revealed in the late 1990s that market makers on Nasdaq routinely manipulated the supply of stock and spreads to their advantage.)

Dad taught me to look for patterns in trading. He told me that in down markets, buyers tend to push stocks up in the morning, while those looking to sell would hold out and then dump at the end of the day, hoping to get a higher price—a piece of wisdom subsequently confirmed by a number of technical analysts. I learned from him how to plow through monthly reports on insiders' stock trades for advance warning signs that something was afoot in a company. Of course, the next task was to find out what was afoot. Dad, as always, looking for ways to tie his economic theories to daily life, did not give me an allowance; instead, he gave me a "salary" that varied according to how well my research paid off in the market and how well I did at school.

One of my earliest memories of these adventures in investing involved the bonds of bankrupt railroads. We looked for value in railroad bonds, where the stigma of bankruptcy and no income made the bonds cheap in terms of what investors could expect from reorganization.

At first I earned my "salary" by reading stock quotes. Later, Dad put me to work sifting through a book on railroad assets and debt written by the legendary analyst Patrick B. McGinnis for the bond firm Pflugfelder, Bampton, and Rust. The job was tedious, but patience was rewarded when we came upon bonds selling at deep discounts to what one could ultimately get for the underlying assets, even in bankruptcy. Although I hated school, I loved doing research with my father.

Dad finished writing his book in the mid-1930s but could not find a publisher. This was not surprising, since he was an unknown writer with no degree in economics, venturing into broad assertions about the nature of economics with a boldness that might have given Adam Smith pause. Undeterred, he published the book himself. The years since have validated much of his thinking. His approach to profits was far ahead of its time and was replicated independently in the 1930s by Polish economist Michal Kalecki (who might have been more influential had he not published only in Polish). When Dad was devising his system, figures for national income had not yet come into vogue, but he was essentially describing gross national product.

Although they may have focused on the same numbers, my father and Kalecki had very different viewpoints. Kalecki was a socialist who believed that unemployment was inevitable under capitalism; Dad believed that capitalism gave workers the most freedom of choice and that if the government ran correctly, there could be full employment. My brother Jay wrote a paper recently pointing out that if analysts looked at Europe in the 1990s, they would think Kalecki was right, but if they looked at the United States in the same period, they would think Dad was right.

More recently, the late economist Hyman Minsky gave some credit to Dad's work, particularly his ability to see how prosperity leads to its own decline by ultimately producing speculative excesses. As good times roll along, people lose sight of risk (and often justify the change with talk of a "new economy"). Eventually, these excesses lead to a point where people can't meet their obligations, and the bad times begin. From his vantage point in the hereafter, Dad would be shocked at the lack of social progress.

It never occurred to me that there was any other proper way of looking at the economy. Other views were just wrong. Even so, Dad's book was and is heavy going. Dutifully, as a teenager I started reading it, but I bogged down in the book's thicket of equations and dense prose. I have to admit, I've never finished it. I learned an enormous amount from Dad, but it was more from dinner-table conversation than from his writing.

Although he focused on his economics, Dad had whimsy as well. Once when he was walking the family mutt in Riverside Park, he happened upon a woman walking some splendid pedigreed pooch. When she asked what breed our dog happened to be, without hesitation Dad replied that we had a Uruguayan Jaguar Hound, a singularly rare dog.

In the summers, I went off to camp or to a house we rented on the Jersey shore. When I was sixteen, I toured the country with a group of students from high schools and colleges in the East. I was probably the only student on the tour who asked for word on investments in his letters home. In one letter from Chicago, I spent more time discussing the merits of the *Chicago Journal of Commerce*, as compared to *The Wall Street Journal*, than I did the wonders of Lake Michigan. From Yosemite National Park I wrote that it was a beautiful place, but I was also interested in the beauties of Merit Chapman, a maritime service company. In my letter home, I wrote,

"Today I saw the first financial page in weeks. I think that we should definitely get into Merit Chapman. The records show the boys have been buying it in and the recent strength, in my opinion, proves they will pay accumulations [on the preferred stock]."

I attended Townsend Harris High School in Manhattan. Although it was a public school, entry depended on your relative standing in a competitive examination. Indeed, at that time, it was more prestigious than the Bronx High School of Science and Stuyvesant High School. Although I did well on the exam, my grades never matched my supposed aptitude.

This underachievement continued when I went on to City College. Having endured lectures from my father on my poor grades in high school, I knew I had to do something when I saw the mediocre grades I received the first term. In a flash of inspiration, I went to university records and looked up my father's grades from the class of 1901 (or "naughty one" as it was nicknamed). As luck would have it, his grades were no better than mine. These I produced with a flourish along with my report. He still managed to have the last word. As he perused his mediocre report card, he remarked, "They must have confused me with Chester Arthur Levy."

My time at CCNY did produce one other satisfying moment. After taking an economics course, I applied to take a class in advanced securities analysis with the same professor, Joe Taffet. He turned me down, either because I was too argumentative or because my grades were not good enough. Two years after graduation, the school contacted me and asked me to teach this very course, which I did for a number of years.

My first thoughts about the role of psychology in the markets began to take shape when World War II broke out in Europe in September 1939 as Hitler invaded Poland. There had been many rumors of war in the months before, and on each rumor, the market would tank. When war became a fact, however, the market soared as investors grabbed for stocks in heavy industry, defense, sugar, and aircraft—industries that had done well in World War I. Although the world had changed enormously since 1918, everyone seemed to envision this war as a replay of the Great War. It was not, of course, and stocks that skyrocketed at the outset of war ultimately did very poorly. For his part, Dad sold all his war-related stocks at the outset and bought shares of retail companies, particularly chains and department stores, such as National Department Stores, Interstate Department Stores, and Federated Department Stores, which did spectacularly well. His reasoning was that there would be no market for war-related materials after the war was over, but there would be huge demand for retail products from consumers flush with war profits, who had not had the opportunity to buy goods during the war because of rationing.

Dad's one mistake was thinking the war would be short. I had a particularly horrible report card in 1940 and waited for the right moment to bring it to my parents. That moment came when I heard over the radio that Hitler had invaded Belgium, Holland, and France. Knowing that Dad would be glued to the radio, I rushed in and got my mother to sign the card. I remember my father saying that the invasion was "the last act of a desperate man." Of course, the war lasted another five years.

The unexpected turns of stocks during World War II offered a lesson about a fundamental frailty in forecasts of the market and the economy. All we can ever do is look at the past to predict the future, but life is dynamic and constantly changing, so the assumptions governing predictions are bound to be wrong. Instead, Dad tried to look at the situation structurally: Given new circumstances, where were profits likely to flow? What companies were well positioned to take advantage of the situation, and what were they worth? Essentially,

Dad was engaged in value investing, the approach first described by Benjamin Graham and then followed by his student Warren Buffett.

In some respects, all investing is value investing. Anyone who buys a stock has some picture of what the company might be worth at some future time. The question is whether the expected returns are sufficiently greater than risk-free investments, such as Treasury bonds, to warrant taking some risk. Everybody works this out over time, and that risk premium varies with the mood of a particular period. In the 1930s, the expectation of a 15 percent return would have wowed investors; during the irrational exuberance of the late 1990s, the same return was regarded as humdrum.

As the war wound down in 1945, I was drafted. After basic training at Camp Blanding in Jacksonville, Florida, I was sent to Germany, where I was assigned to a combat engineering corps in Berlin charged with the rebuilding of Templehof Airport. Eager to learn more about Germany in this period immediately after its surrender, I asked for a transfer to OMGUS—the Office of Military Government (U.S.)—specifically to the office responsible for fine arts and monuments.

It may seem odd given the horrors Germany perpetrated during the war, but my postwar tour of duty in Germany was not a bad time. I was independent and immensely curious about this nation. Optimistic by nature (I inherited this from Dad), I spent a good deal of time trying to get to know the Germans.

Still, every now and then, like a whisper from the grave, an odd comment or moment would forcefully remind me of the horrors of German anti-Semitism. Once when I was talking to a young German woman, she casually remarked, "You speak German like a Jew." Needless to say, that comment ended our conversation.

I thought a lot about how such evil could come from the many decent people I met. In one of my letters home, I wrote, "I believe now that there is no relation between the actions of a nation and the actions of the individual. I have met pleasant and kind people here of every nationality. But to quote Albert Einstein, 'Nationalism is the measles of civilization.'"

While the GIs were living well in Berlin, it's hard to imagine the poverty and struggle of the average German, who among other hardships barely had enough to eat. The enormous privation around me started me thinking that one of the prerequisites of real freedom is money. Money gives you choices, and in an unregulated society the choices were unlimited. So was the corruption which was everywhere. Everybody played the black market. A carton of cigarettes paid for at the PX with occupation marks (the currency issued while Germany was being stabilized) could be sold on the street for vast sums of money. Proof of the ubiquity of such dealings was that at the end of their tours, the men in my unit still had all the occupation marks they had been issued, ostensibly implying that no one had spent any money. I too bartered my cigarettes, but I was shocked by the greed of those who did it on a much larger scale—such as officers who would requisition Leica cameras to resell.

Apart from corruption and misery, the air was charged with intrigue. Maneuvering by the Allies to carve up Europe was well under way by the time I arrived in Germany, with the Russians clearly being the fastest out of the box. I was outraged by the crude and open way in which the Russians violated the Potsdam Agreement, expropriating vast quantities of German goods, and when they did pay for something, they used American occupation marks that they printed on American plates. They openly fired civilians put into positions by Americans and replaced them with German communist sympathizers. Everybody hated the Russians, including the German communists. Nevertheless, when I first met some Russian officers socially, I was completely charmed.

The Russians had challenged the Americans to a chess match, and I managed to get the last spot on the American team during an elimination match to choose the lineup. I played a Russian captain, and when I resigned an only slightly inferior position, we became buddies and started playing for fun. Another Russian expert came to our table and gave me a few tips on how to beat my former adversary.

The French and the British came to watch the proceedings, amazed that the Russians had attended a social function. To my new Russian friend's surprise, I told him that what small support for communism there was in America came not from the proletariat but from the intelligentsia. Later during the toasts, we told the Russians gently that chess may be their game, but let them try to compete with us in business—that was our game.

Even while I was in Germany, I never lost my interest in the markets. In one note to my brother Jay, I wrote: "As you may not realize being so close to it, securities are selling way above any intrinsic value they could possibly have. So at the first indication of a change on the trend of profits, sell!! Remember '38." In this short note is the essence of the approach to investing I learned from Dad.

3

The Right Time

I WASN'T SURE WHAT I wanted to do after Uncle Sam decided he no longer needed my services. Music was out since I had no talent, despite my love of the piano. I toyed with the idea of starting an import business, but I was more interested in investing. My father arranged an interview for me at the brokerage house of Hirsch and Company, where he had an account. To a young man just starting out, this seemed to be a very large firm, with several offices in Manhattan as well as in Geneva and Paris, but in reality, it was in the middle of the pack. And so, in 1948, I began my career on Wall Street as a junior research analyst. The offices were at 25 Broad Street, in the heart of the financial district. In those days, securities were delivered by hand, and thus it was useful to have investment companies clustered together.

There was nothing momentous about that first job. People tend to fret too much about getting their first job — is it the right fit, is the pay right? — when the important thing is just to get out and work.

Their first job is unlikely to be their last. I suspect that it is easier for people to discover what they really want to do if they just do something.

Wall Street remained out of favor because of the many lives ruined by the crash and the Great Depression. Many of the smartest guys tended to go into government—recall Franklin Roosevelt's brain trust—or otherwise climb the corporate ladder. Much of my competition consisted of shell-shocked veterans of the 1930s. Wall Street was also a good place to dump the dimmer sons of prosperous families. Protected by fixed commissions and long-standing relationships with investment banking clients, these princelings had to be true imbeciles to fail as the market continued to recover from the Great Depression in the post–World War II boom. People did not need to be unduly nimble to make money on Wall Street—unless they were outsiders without establishment connections to family money and the "old boy network."

That was the rub. At that time, bright young Jews were limited as to where they could go on Wall Street. There were Catholic firms (e.g., Merrill Lynch), WASP firms (Brown Brothers; Harriman; White, Weld), and a few Jewish firms (Goldman Sachs; Lehman Brothers). These firms would do business with each other but tended to hire their own kind. Morgan Stanley was not only WASP but Princeton as well. It helped to have family connections, too.

Indeed, Wall Street was at that time the most aristocratic business in America. Since capital for a firm could come only from a partner's family, firms were routinely passed along to sons. Being a member of this privileged club in the early 1950s carried about the same risk of financial failure as being a nephew of the king of Saudi Arabia in the mid-1970s.

Although America was poised for a great boom, most people did not know it. When I joined Wall Street, we were in the middle of the longest bear market of the post–World War II period. It began in 1946 and continued to 1949, and even then it would be another sixteen months before prices recovered to 1946 levels. The bear market was a gift of the Federal Reserve Board, which had raised margin requirements to 100 percent to head off a speculative frenzy after the war. It is difficult to overestimate the degree to which the psychological legacy of the Depression weighed upon the market in those days. Memories of the role of margin debt in the 1929 crash were fresh in people's minds. The Fed not only raised margin requirements from 40 percent to 100 percent, which forced speculators to sell stock to meet margin calls, but it also imposed a regulation that sellers of stock who had margin debt could use the proceeds of the sale only to further reduce that debt. This knocked the Dow Jones Industrial Average down by about 25 percent in the span of three months.

The investment climate was deeply conservative, as the markets were burdened with both legislation and attitudes that limited opportunities. Trust funds in New York State could at best keep only 25 percent of their holdings in stocks, but most trustees opted to stash their entire portfolio in bonds.

The logic of this analysis was that stocks are inherently more risky than bonds and thus should provide holders with a "risk premium." This premium would compensate for the fact that bonds have a guaranteed price at maturity, that bonds must pay their coupon (a dividend is discretionary), and that bonds have a higher claim on the assets of a company in the event of bankruptcy. It also shows that nobody then worried about inflation.

Those who did trade stocks were few and did so rarely. In the 1950s, only 5 percent of Americans owned stocks, in contrast to over 50 percent who own stocks today. Tape watchers had to be a particularly patient breed then, as Dow Jones computed its industrial average only once every hour, and even then it was often late.

There were far fewer stocks than today, and they traded far less frequently. Daily volume was measured in the hundreds of thousands of shares traded, in contrast to today's hundreds of millions. (There are 100 times more shares listed today than there were in 1955.) In the early 1950s, roughly 15 to 20 percent of the shares on the New York Stock Exchange traded each year, as opposed to roughly 106 percent turnover today.

I entered Wall Street when people were more afraid of risks than they were eager for profits. During the next five decades, I saw these attitudes shift dramatically. The pattern running through these shifts was that avarice gradually overcame fear of risks until investors put aside reason and caution as they chased dreams of wealth, a transition that set the stage for the next crash and a renewed appreciation of risk. Certainly, fear still ruled the day when I entered the market, creating perhaps the ideal psychological situation for the market boom of the next fifteen years.

For one thing, stocks were undervalued, not only shares of bankrupt companies and intricate reorganizations or spin-offs, but also large retailers such as Montgomery Ward and Sears Roebuck. I remember that Sewell Avery, head of Montgomery Ward, was convinced that the United States would sink into depression again, and thus he refused to invest the company's pile of cash. Sears's management, surveying the same landscape, saw the evolution of shopping centers as the future and invested in out-of-town stores. Sears became a giant, and Montgomery Ward became history. The big established brokerage firms could profitably focus on mainstream companies and ignore complicated and obscure situations. This created great opportunities for the enterprising and diligent analyst.

My starting pay was $150 per month, about 1/100th the pay of junior analysts at the peak of the 1990s bull market (although I was promised a substantial raise if things worked out). Unfortunately, the research department at Hirsch was something less than a shining beacon for the rest of the investment community. My role at first was somewhat similar to the diminished role of analysts today: providing a rationale to generate commissions and business for the firm.

I had different goals. I wanted to unearth undervalued gems, to find value in places ignored or misunderstood by other analysts. I wanted to make money with money. To that end, I focused on companies with small market capitalizations, believing that other analysts would be likely to ignore them.

Almost from the beginning, I was frustrated. I knew I could make more money by investing in the market myself than as a broker or analyst. Moreover, I was one of the few at Hirsch who knew anything about evaluating securities. But as the most junior analyst whose responsibilities included answering mail, I had a hard time getting others at Hirsch interested in my reports.

Rather than stew, I turned my frustrations into something useful. I met Robert Bleiberg, the editor of *Barron's*, through a friend who had been a class ahead of me at Townsend Harris. Bleiberg agreed to let me write articles, either unsigned or under the pseudonym of Noel Samuelson. (Noel is Leon spelled backward, and Samuelson was my mother's maiden name.) This led to one of those satisfying moments we all fantasize about but rarely get a chance to savor.

For an astute investor, the worst situation is an "efficient market," in which all information is known and understood by all players and in which prices accurately reflect that information. Not to worry— none of us will ever see that. Instead, the factors that create opportunity are emotions such as fear, which can drive prices far below fair value, and changes that create unknowns, which can flummox those players trying to outfox the market. In the latter case, investors have a great ally in government, whose attempts to legislate fairness or improve the workings of the markets almost always create opportunities and special situations for investors.

One such example was the Public Utilities Holding Company Act, a legacy of the Great Depression championed by Franklin D. Roosevelt to break the monopolistic power of utility holding companies. The act forced utilities to spin off various subsidiaries, but these emerging companies were often extremely difficult to evaluate. The holding company structure (disallowed by the PUHCA) was based on an enormous amount of leverage. The holding company Commonwealth & Southern (at one time chaired by Wendell Willkie) had subsidiaries, including Ohio Edison and the Southern Company. These "subs" in turn held assets of operating companies. Under the PUHCA, each shareholder of Commonwealth & Southern would get shares in Ohio Edison and Southern Company, allowing the diligent analyst to evaluate the assets against the price of the stock.

One company spun off by the centrifugal force of the PUHCA was American & Foreign Power. Forced to restructure by the act, it issued new subordinated debentures as well as common stock. It was a difficult company to value in part because of its far-flung assets (including such companies as Argentine Electric Power), but my research led me to believe that it was worth more than it was then priced in the marketplace. My colleagues at Hirsch were not interested in my analysis, and so I published my findings in *Barron's* as Noel Samuelson. Shortly after the article appeared, the head of research stopped by my office, dropped the issue of *Barron's* on my desk, and said, "Now, Leon, this guy Samuelson knows what he's talking about." In retrospect, it is clear that one of the most dependable ways to make a fortune in the postwar years was through close scrutiny of the dozens of companies spun off as a result of the PUHCA.

Perhaps because business was slow, Dan Pierce, the partner in charge of retail sales at Hirsch, offered to let me sell my research to anyone willing to open an account at Hirsch, but my commission was pegged at 25 percent of the business I brought in, as opposed to the 33 percent set for regular customers' account reps. I quickly noticed that the 8 percent difference between the two rates was greater than my monthly salary. In essence, by allowing me to trade at this discounted rate, Hirsch was getting an analyst for free. I made my feelings known to Pierce but to no avail.

Thus I was inordinately interested when I heard other rumblings of discontent at Hirsch. One of the most successful salesmen in the office was a broker named Max Oppenheimer, a tall, slim, bespectacled immigrant who spoke English with a thick German accent. Max had been a cigar salesman in Würzburg, Germany, and when he fled from Hitler, he maintained strong contacts with the Jewish refugee community.

Max had on occasion bought the stocks I recommended and had made money. His dissatisfaction had to do with Hirsch's policy against trading in sperrmarks (German marks given to people as reparations for property confiscated by the Nazis). Sperrmarks could be spent in Germany but were not convertible into other currencies. Max was constantly running into refugees in New York who wanted to exchange their sperrmarks for dollars. Since an investment company could put those marks to work in Germany, Max saw the opportunity to profit by making a market in sperrmarks in the United States.

Hirsch hewed to its policy, a decision I thought driven by a touch of snobbery about dealing with Max's refugee clients, as well as practicality. Converting sperrmarks was a laborious process; each transaction involved notifying banks and calling people. But because Max was a valued employee, the partners let him set up his own separate company in a glass-walled boardroom on the Hirsch premises. Entrepreneur that he was, Max found a dentist willing to lend him his seat on the New York Stock Exchange, and with $100,000 in mostly borrowed capital, Max and two partners set up Oppenheimer and Company. With no rent and no back-office expense, Oppenheimer was successful from the beginning. Max did not even have to invest in a ticker, since the glass wall looked out on Hirsch's tape.

Intrigued with this new company, I sent Max and his partners a huge bouquet and a note wishing them good luck. They were more pleased than I ever might have expected. Some months later, the gesture paid off when they asked me to join the firm as a partner.

On my twenty-sixth birthday, having invested $12,500 of my own money (about one-quarter of my net worth at the time), I joined Oppenheimer and Company in 1951 as a partner and its director of research. I knew going in that I would be making less money than at Hirsch, but more important, I was putting myself in a position that offered far more opportunity. Years later I came upon an insight of Henry Kissinger's that captured the essence of strategic positioning. He wrote in A *World Restored*, his book about the Congress of Vienna, that mediocre diplomats will always sacrifice long-term advantage for a short-term improvement in their position. For all its frustrations, or perhaps because of them, that first job at Hirsch had the inestimable value of helping me discover what I really wanted to do.

Besides Max, the other partners were two Germans, Hugo Heksch and Albert Deuble. Oppenheimer also had three secretaries, two of whom detested each other. At times during these early years, such was the ubiquity of Germans at Oppenheimer that my secretary Marni Cone and I referred to ourselves as the English-Speaking Union. After the market closed at noon on Saturdays, my partners and I would lunch at Luchow's, a legendary New York restaurant that my late friend Ben Sonnenberg, the great public relations impresario, once described as the only German restaurant with a Chinese name.

Six months after I joined Oppenheimer, we had a Christmas party with food supplied by one of the firm's customers who owned a delicatessen. Though ours was a tiny firm, Max upheld the class system and reserved the turkey sandwiches for partners. Max, sparing no expense, also told us he had hired an orchestra to entertain us at the party. The "orchestra" was a one-man band with a complicated apparatus that allowed him to play the harmonica, accordion, drums, and other instruments simultaneously. From its outset, then, Oppenheimer was not a typical Wall Street firm.

As a one-man research department running on a shoestring budget, I could not compete with the giant Wall Street firms, but we still had to keep up appearances. I remember that Goldman Sachs had published a report on the Denver and Rio Grande Railroad that I wanted to see. When the obliging Goldman research department told me they would hold a copy, I said, "Great, I'll send over a messenger." Thereupon I donned my raincoat and headed around the corner to 40 Wall Street.

At that time, research in general was in a sorry state. As an ambitious young man, I set myself a high standard and made a point of not publishing a report on a company if none of us had visited its offices and interviewed its executives. Because of an inherent shyness, however, I had a rocky start putting this policy into practice.

One of my first targets was the shipping company Moore McCormack, because it was in an industry that at the time benefited from an array of subsidies and protections and was selling at a very low multiple of earnings and yield. I arranged a meeting with the executive vice president, but when I entered his office, I froze. After a couple of minutes of awkward silence, he said, "I've had analysts who asked me dumb questions, and I've had analysts come in here and ask smart questions. But I have never until now met an analyst who asked me no questions."

Max plumbed every opportunity to bring in new customers. Oppenheimer advertised my reports in *Der Aufbau*, the German-refugee newspaper published in New York, and when someone called or wrote in, the lead would be handed to a broker. Max recruited the refugees who came to the firm to trade sperrmarks as well. Everywhere he went, Max sought out the German refugee community, and we eventually came to dread his trips, because every time he returned, he would open a new office. We could track Max's movements as Oppenheimer offices sprang up in Frankfurt, Cannes, Buenos Aires, Montevideo, and São Paulo.

The German emphasis also extended to our investments. Having grown up in Germany, Max was attuned to opportunities deriving from the Alien Properties Custodians Act, legislation that authorized the selling off of German holdings in the United States that had been seized during World War II. Some of the assets we investigated belonged to notorious giants like I. G. Farben.

While investigating one company being sold off under this legislation, I had an epiphany that sealed my conviction that I had chosen the right path for myself. The company was Associated Telephone and Telegraph, a foreign subsidiary of the telephone conglomerate Theodore Gary, an American holding company. It was a monster to evaluate because of its diverse holdings, but I set about constructing a consolidated balance sheet. This was not an easy task, and I worked long hours into the night on the project. As I dug deeper into the company, I realized that its share price was little more than its annual earnings—a huge opportunity for the company that successfully bid for its assets.

For the first time, as I looked around the dim, empty office, I realized that my only limitations were my own, not my partners'. I was as much in control of my destiny as it was possible to be. I was elated.

But my mood was soon deflated by the fate of my report. I convinced my partners of the hidden value of the company, but we could marshal only a few million dollars, not enough to make a serious bid in the eyes of the alien-property custodian. Therefore, I decided that if we could not win the prize ourselves, we might find a richer bidder and still pocket a finder's fee. I showed the report to principals at Graham and Newman, the business home of Benjamin Graham, under the assumption that they would understand the logic of my analysis.

They did, and offered a winning bid for the company that ultimately netted them a profit of several million dollars. For a finder's fee, Mickey Newman, Graham's partner, sent me a check for $250. I was so angry that I threatened to sue. Newman upped the fee to $1,000, sufficient to stop me from going to court but still well short of the 1 or 2 percent that a finder might expect for the long hours that went into unearthing an opportunity like Associated Telephone and Telegraph.

I was annoyed, but I had no reason to believe that Ben Graham himself was in any way involved in his company's attempt to stiff me. Indeed, Newman would not let me meet Graham, who divided his time between his firm and his duties as a professor at Columbia University. (At Columbia, one of his students, a young man named Warren Buffett, took his lessons very much to heart, and proved the merit of value investing in his extraordinary four-decade run at the helm of Berkshire Hathaway.)

Value investing is an approach to stocks that is as close as it gets to a golden rule. After all, an analyst researching a stock is only trying to estimate what the underlying company will be worth to an individual owner at some point in the future. It's a simple idea but devilishly difficult in the execution, because so many variables weigh upon a company's future value. An evaluation of its assets depends on management, conditions at that moment, and the market's attitude toward the industry. Management changes, personality clashes, changing technologies and tastes, access to credit, foreign and domestic competition, economic factors such as interest rates, access to raw materials or talent, changes in tax policy—the list goes on and on—all affect an appraisal of value.

Typically, analysts evaluating the future prospects of a company look at its past. Where else can they look, after all? And yet, even if they had a perfect snapshot of the past, they would be mistaken to assume that the conditions that held in the past will hold in the present or future.

Perhaps this is why the more recent notion of a perfect market—an "efficient market"—in which current prices reflect all available information, is so seductive. A perfect market assumes that prices reflect all prior research at that point. Those who believe in an efficient market, and I am not one of them, believe that stocks can never be underpriced or markets overvalued. They say you can't beat an efficient market—all you need to do is put your money into an index fund. The problem is that all the stocks may be reasonably priced compared to one another, but the whole market may be too high or too low.

The market may not be efficient, but over time it is pretty efficient, especially at grinding down the egos of those who succumb to the temptation of seeing profits as certification of their own genius. In an uncertain world, governed by probabilities rather than rules, the only constant may be that the more time that passes, the more probable it becomes that you will at some point encounter an improbable event.

It is, of course, possible to believe that the market is unpre-

dictable but that investors still can profit from its moves. My friend
Charles Stevenson is a trader who devised a system of investing that
he compares to sailing. Charles spent hours in the library in the
1970s studying the price movements of commodities. He likens the
market to the weather in the sense that you may know that conditions for storms are favorable, but still find it impossible to predict
where and when these storms will arise and where they will travel. In
Charles's view, however, you can determine the wind and sail with it
until you detect that it is changing, whereupon you set a new course.

Charles followed this view very profitably by betting on the rise in
silver prices when brothers Nelson Bunker Hunt and William Herbert Hunt tried to corner the market. He detected the wind was
changing before the Hunts did, however, and he exited with a huge
profit, while the Hunt brothers lost a fortune. It has been said that if
you follow the crowd and know when to get out, you will do very
well, regardless of the logic that governs the crowd's movements.

My approach is different. To be sure, I want to see where the
crowd is going. But then I try to appraise how changing conditions
might affect crowd behavior. If I think the economy is poised for a
severe downturn, I will try to anticipate its effect on the crowd and
try to invest accordingly. This, of course, is what Dad did when he
tried to anticipate which companies would benefit after the end of
World War II.

I never thought a perfect market existed. Although I am aware of
the pitfalls and complexities of estimating the future value of a company, I believe it is possible to make an informed estimate as to the
likelihood of a company's success or failure. Today it is also possible
to invest by making decisions based on the probable movements of
markets rather than investing in stocks of individual companies.

Following such a strategy was not possible in 1951 because there
were no index options or futures in which to invest. Nor was there

an efficient-market theory, which was not developed until the late 1960s. In 1951 the markets were heavily regulated, and the dissemination of information was slow and spotty at best.

But these conditions still offered abundant opportunities for profit to investors who knew where to look for them. I tend to discount the lip service that corporate executives pay to free trade and markets. Once companies have access to markets, they immediately start pouring vast amounts of money into lobbying efforts to convince politicians to erect new barriers to keep others out. Textile and media companies have pursued this most aggressively in recent years, the textile companies seeking tariffs on cheaper imports, and the media companies seeking to maintain their hold on the public airwaves. Businesspeople who often sound like libertarians when markets are going up suddenly sound like socialists and beg for bailouts and protection from governments when the economy heads south.

In 1951 as a research analyst I scoured monthly reports on insider stock trades for signs of activity that might point me in the direction of a promising opportunity. Today this would be much more difficult. For every analyst looking for undervalued companies in 1951, there are probably ten doing so today. I also realized that people often repeat themselves, and therefore if I studied the moves of astute investors, I could figure out what they were going to do next.

So I studied the purchases and sales of corporate officers and directors, which had to be reported to the SEC and were a matter of public record. This led me to appreciate the virtuosity of two maestros of investing, the well-known J. Paul Getty and the virtually unknown Sy Scheuer, both of whom understood how to exploit the vagaries of the stock market to gradually gain control of vastly undervalued assets. Unlike today's financiers, who want instant returns, these men had extraordinary patience as well as the ability to conceive and execute complicated plans that in some cases took decades to bring to fruition.

One major problem in investing is how long it takes for things to happen. All specialists have a time frame that they believe is important—the astrophysicist who thinks in terms of billions of years can't put himself in the mind of the meteorologist who thinks about the future in terms of hours and days. Both will be befuddled by the archaeologist whose time scale spans less that that of the astrophysicist but more than the meteorologist. The outer edge of the time horizon for Wall Street analysts today might be a year. These differences may account for the way people on Wall Street so often talk past each other. I will say, "Consolidated Chicken Feed is a great stock," and a colleague will ask, "Will it have losses the next quarter?" But I don't care about the next quarter—I'm looking at strategic and demographic factors that will favor the industry and this company over the next few years, and sometimes the next decade.

When it comes to visionary long-term investors, perhaps no one operated on a grander scale than John Paul Getty. Figuring out where the wily oil man was going was no easy task; his strategy was so complicated that I doubt even the brokers executing his trades had much clue of his overall design. For me, Getty offered a case study of how to implement a long-term strategy.

By the 1930s, Getty realized he could acquire oil far more cheaply by buying the undervalued stock of companies that held known reserves than he could by drilling, with all the guesswork and risks that wildcatting entailed. He also knew the depressed shares of other companies offered an economical way to add refining and marketing capacity to his oil company. Perhaps most impressive, Getty recognized it would take years to implement this strategy of acquisitions. Still, he managed to pull it off artfully under the noses of investors and competitors who could have thwarted his ambitions at any moment.

Getty's opportunity arose in 1934 when, as one of the final details of the government-mandated breakup of John D. Rockefeller's Standard Oil Company, Mission Corporation was formed to hold substantial shares of two other oil companies—Tidewater Associated Oil Company, which had refineries and marketing capacity, and Skelly Oil, which had substantial reserves. The shares of Mission were distributed to Standard Oil stockholders. Tidewater's large refinery in Naples, Italy, was then running at only 55 percent capacity, and the price of the company's shares was depressed. Getty saw his opportunity in this undervalued company, and through Pacific Western Oil Company, which Getty controlled, he began purchasing shares in both Tidewater and Mission. By 1937 he had control of Mission and about 20 percent of Tidewater. Through Mission, Getty continued to buy Tidewater, while he used his substantial block of Tidewater stock to thwart other suitors who had their eye on the company.

Getty was a legendary cheapskate (in Kuwait he was appalled to discover that the toilets in his facilities were using fresh water and ordered that the plumbing run henceforth on sea water), but he was not without a sense of humor. Once while visiting the Tidewater refinery in Naples, he took time off to stop by the National Archaeological Museum. The museum was known for its collection of ancient art, including Roman portrait busts. The Republican school of sculpture, popular before the reign of Augustus, the first Roman emperor, favored realistic depictions, which showed the subjects warts and all, rather than the more idealized images of Greek sculpture or later Roman imperial sculpture. As he passed one bust, Getty said, "There's my good friend Joe Skelly!" (in fact, Skelly was his mortal enemy), and a little later he saw another bust that he said resembled the head of Tidewater Oil. There in the museum halls were displayed the heads that would roll as Getty completed his strategy for building his oil company.

This chess match entered its slow-motion endgame in 1948 when Getty deployed a new strategy to gain control of Tidewater. Mission Corporation formed Mission Development Corporation and transferred all of Mission's accumulated Tidewater stock to the new company. To conserve cash, Getty persuaded Lehman Brothers to underwrite an exchange, offering new Tidewater preferred stock for shares of Tidewater common stock.

The offer also served another purpose. By exchanging Mission stock for Tidewater, Getty increased his percentage ownership of the remaining Tidewater equity without paying a premium. This ploy, called the "shrink," is a marvelous way investors can increase their share in a company without putting up any money. The reason more financiers don't use the shrink is that it requires great patience and stealth.

By 1950, Getty owned 45 percent of Tidewater stock, which effectively gave him control of the company. With control of Tidewater, Mission and Mission Development had served their purpose, and he ultimately merged them into Getty Oil. Even before I joined Oppenheimer, I had watched this drama unfold, having pieced together Getty's plan from my reading of insider purchases in SEC reports. As a steady buyer of Mission stock, I went along for the ride (and wrote an article for *The Financial World*, a small financial magazine). As for Getty, he not only acquired the pieces of his oil empire, but his trips to Naples gave him a taste for ancient art as well. He became acquainted with an archaeologist who had helped excavate Herculaneum, an ancient Roman city that was covered in lava from the eruption of Mount Vesuvius, who then accompanied Getty on a trip to Herculaneum and showed him the ancient Villa Papyri, which was then being uncovered. Getty was struck by the grace and elegance of this villa, and it served as the model for the original Getty Museum constructed to house his art collection in Malibu, California.

Whereas Getty had a global reputation, perhaps the most creative and brilliant investor I ever encountered could have walked down any street on the planet without being recognized. This was Sy Scheuer, who did everything he could to keep his name out of the papers and financial journals. Whereas Getty's play was oil, Scheuer's masterstroke was an immensely complicated series of moves that involved coal and, more important, the barges and railroads that moved it. I noticed him because the insider trading reports revealed his growing position in West Virginia Coal and Coke.

Of all the deals I've witnessed on Wall Street, Scheuer's play was the most interesting. It did not involve strong-arm tactics or dubious moves. It did involve brilliant use of the tax laws and a great strategy. And, like Getty, Scheuer was a virtuoso in his use of the shrink. In this one deal, Scheuer made a fortune.

Scheuer first made money as a feather merchant in Argentina, and then in real estate in New York. He started acquiring West Virginia Coal and Coke, once the privately owned business of the family of composer Cole Porter, in the early 1950s. The moribund company was then perceived as a dying coal business. Scheuer realized, however, that the coal company camouflaged a thriving barge company, the largest in the United States, whose value was nowhere near reflected in the company's market value of roughly $6 million. By 1954, Scheuer owned 44 percent and had control of the undervalued company, but he preferred to operate in the shadows, and the SEC required registration once individual holdings in a company topped 10 percent. Years later, his son Wally told me that Sy bought stock on behalf of each of his five children, making sure that none of them held more than 9.9 percent. Eventually, his accountant convinced Sy to divulge his holdings. Getting control was just the beginning of a series of shrewd moves, as Scheuer managed to get his acquisitions to finance his great game, and he pulled off his audacious market play right under the noses of Wall Street.

Scheuer acquired his shares at prices ranging between $10 and $14 a share. The stock then paid a dividend of $1.20 a year. Among his first moves, he cut and then passed this dividend. A few years later, he paid a dividend—not as a distribution of profits but, he claimed, as a return on capital, which would be nontaxable. He argued that the dividend did not represent funds the company had earned. Only the federal government could decide this, and the company immediately sought an IRS ruling. This took several years because the parties had to go back to the early years of the century and reconstruct the company's pre–World War I descent into bankruptcy in order to prove his case.

This battle was only the teaser for a much more ambitious plan. Once he had his favorable ruling, Scheuer launched a series of complicated maneuvers. The Ohio River Company, the barge company wholly owned by West Virginia Coal and Coke, had a number of contracts with utilities to deliver coal to places as far away as New Orleans. The problem was that these barges returned empty. So Scheuer sought out and signed long-term contracts to deliver coal to utilities on the return trips.

Scheuer realized that these long-term contracts made the barge company a de facto utility, and the contracts gave him something he could borrow against, since the banks could count on a predictable return. Armed with his government ruling, he convinced management to mortgage the barge company to the hilt, and then pay cash to the shareholders as return on capital. The company complied, and Scheuer and other shareholders reaped a windfall in the form of a nontaxable dividend of $25 per share on a stock that was trading in the low teens. Along with other shareholders, I was thrilled.

Scheuer's next move was to sell off the coal company for a large tax loss. He then offered the Ohio River Company to Eastern Gas and Fuel for an exchange of stock. Assisting Scheuer in this endeavor was a brilliant man named Eli Goldstone, who helped Scheuer charm the board of Eastern Gas. Eastern had been part of the large conglomerate Kopper's United, and it was one of the utilities spun off under Roosevelt's Public Utility Holding Company Act.

After convincing Eastern Gas's executives that the exchange was in their interest (it also made Scheuer the largest shareholder in Eastern Gas), Goldstone set about convincing the board that Scheuer was a sleepy old man who wouldn't cause any trouble as a board member. At the very first meeting, Scheuer had been warned not to mention the company plane, which in those days was a greater luxury than it is today. Finally, he could not contain himself. He said he worried about the safety of the chairman of the board, who was so vital to the company, riding around in a small plane. The chairman replied, "I'm glad you brought that up, since I've been thinking of buying a much larger plane."

As had been the case with West Virginia Coal and Coke, once Scheuer controlled Eastern Gas, he had the company continue to buy its own stock. Later, when I got to know Scheuer, he remarked to me, "Leon, if you want a stock to behave, keep buying it." Decades later, Scheuer's insight was confirmed by an academic study of 1,239 companies, which found that those that reduced the supply of stock through repurchases outperformed otherwise equivalent companies that did not. Unfortunately, this lesson has been overlearned and also turned to more short-sighted purposes. Buying-in shares can be a smart tactic if a company is flush with cash and the stock is in the tank. As Warren Buffett once noted, who wouldn't jump at the chance to buy out his partners at 50 cents on the dollar? And of course, as the number of shares being traded shrinks, the percentage of a controlling stake expands.

Buying-in shares is another thing entirely, however, when shares are selling at or near historic highs and priced at many times earnings. Worse is for a company to take on debt in the process, as some companies have done to make the purchases, because when the stock price falls, the company is left with increased debt and diminished capital. In recent years, more and more companies, most notably IBM, have used aggressive share purchases as a device to prop up per-share earnings. If a company buys-in more shares than it issues in a year, per-share earnings rise even if total earnings remain flat, because earnings are being divided by fewer shares.

Among the assets of Eastern Gas and Fuel was a 25 percent stake in the storied railroad Norfolk and Western. Scheuer realized that this holding offered yet another opportunity to increase his control of Eastern at no cost. Using this stake, he offered Eastern Gas and Fuel shareholders one share of Norfolk and Western stock for every two shares of Eastern. As the exchange went through, the company retired the shares that came in, increasing Scheuer's percentage of the company (as well as that of the remaining shareholders) as the number of outstanding shares shrank.

Through the use of the $25 dividend and the shrink, Scheuer reaped a windfall of several hundred million dollars. He did this within the law, although he did play tough. A good deal of the credit for this piece of investment artistry belongs to Scheuer's tax adviser, Harry Silverson of Silverson and Gelberg, who accumulated his own small stake in Eastern along the way. When Silverson died, Scheuer advised the widow of his good friend to sell her shares — at the very time he was accumulating and shrinking the stock. Though a brilliant investor, Scheuer was no Albert Schweitzer.

I followed Scheuer's machinations from afar, through my study of insider reports and what I could glean about the companies he was buying. The research was akin to code breaking or intelligence work. It was impossible to determine the barge company's earnings by examining the annual report of West Virginia Coal and Coke. To do that, I had to dig through filings with the Interstate Commerce Commission. When I did realize there was a diamond buried beneath the company's coal, my colleague Archer Scherl and I published an unsigned article about it in *Barron's*. Moreover, Scheuer got reports from Leo Goldwater, his floor broker at Hettleman and Co., that some people at Oppenheimer were showing an interest in West Virginia Coal and Coke. The last thing Scheuer wanted was publicity and other people spoiling his plan. He urged Goldwater to contact our floor broker to arrange a meeting.

Scheuer was a tall, slim, wiry man in his sixties, more than twice my age. At his apartment on Central Park West, he began the conversation by saying that railroads and coal were terrible businesses. Having done my homework, I told him I knew of a buyer for his shares. This was not the direction that Sy intended the conversation to go. He tried to convince me that everything about my analysis was wrong. But it was right. I suspect Scheuer wanted me to sell him my shares, but when that didn't work, he started giving Oppenheimer some of his family's business. It was the beginning of an association that lasted until he died in 1979. I benefited from his insights into markets, but the secretive and cagey mogul never divulged the details of his investment genius.

Getty and Scheuer were two patient schemers who operated on a grand scale. Deconstructing their plays opened my eyes to the extraordinary discipline, strategic imagination, and perseverance required to unlock and capture the riches lying hidden in the balance sheets of neglected or undervalued corporations. In one sense, these two men were the opposite of accounting wizards at Enron and WorldCom. At these two companies and many other companies today, executives use their understanding of balance sheets to convince the public that revenues are there when they are not and that expenses are not there when they are. Getty and Scheuer, whose reward derived from buying assets at severe discounts, had no interest in prettying up numbers. The two men also offered insight into some of the grating personality traits that often accompany success in the market. But I did not need this particular lesson, since I could find difficult and driven people simply by looking around the Oppenheimer offices.

4

A Galaxy of Financial Talent

As a group, my colleagues at Oppenheimer and Company were, like many Wall Streeters, aggressive and driven. Max Oppenheimer dominated the firm until his death in 1962, and by then we had assembled a team that would bring Oppenheimer far greater growth than Max ever dreamed possible. Luckily, the first and foremost of these key players, Jack Nash, had the ability to manage such an unlikely group.

Jack joined Oppenheimer shortly after I did, as Max's assistant. He was twenty-four years old and a graduate of City College. Born in Berlin, he had fled with his family to Switzerland and then to New York to escape Hitler and his thugs. Jack's great asset was that he had every ability I lacked. He was a solid administrator with a grasp of all the details of managing a growing firm, and he was also a great trader and an astute negotiator. By 1957, Jack became the managing partner of Oppenheimer, and we worked together as partners for almost fifty years. He was the Cerberus of the firm, making sure that none of us crossed any ethical lines, even as pressures mounted and standards relaxed. As long as we were in business together, Jack made sure that our mothers never read anything untoward about us in *The New York Times*.

Jack also had an innate sense of where the market was going on a day-to-day and week-to-week basis. This was a good complement to my perspective, since I tended to ignore the vagaries of the market and pay more attention to searching for areas where value was ignored or undiscovered. As much as anyone, Jack held Oppenheimer together during later periods of spectacular growth that might have torn the company apart.

I had the responsibility of assembling a research department and early on made the decision not to hire anyone who remembered the Depression. This move was cost-effective, since those who remembered the Depression tended to be older and more highly paid. But to some degree, this decision was driven by my feelings about the role of psychology in markets. I reasoned that memories of that devastating market would breed caution where we needed boldness.

I also wanted people who were in the market and had the guts to take risks. My first question was whether a job candidate owned stocks. If he didn't, the interview was over. If he did, I would ask him about his last trade and why he bought or sold a particular stock. Every now and then, a would-be analyst would surprise me with highly original thinking. Over time, we assembled a highly regarded research department.

A number of our early hires came through the recommendations of family and friends. Archer Scherl was a family friend who started in a summer job at Oppenheimer in 1952 while still a student at Ohio State. Over the next thirty years, he worked on and off at Oppenheimer as an analyst, a fund manager, and a banker. The son of a theatrical lawyer, Scherl was a quirky presence in the office, with long hair and open-collared shirts, long before they were fashionable.

We also broke some barriers. Oppenheimer became one of the first investment companies to hire a woman as a securities analyst. This was in 1956, when we hired Frances Heidt. I heard about her from Fred Stein, a very able securities analyst and broker (and whose wife, Sharon Stein, broke some barriers when she became president of Schroeder's Bank). Frances was an ambitious young lady but perhaps not cut out to be an analyst. In the days before sexual harassment became an issue, I asked her out for dinner. She said, "Leon, I can't do this. My father was a union organizer!"

In the years that followed, we hired a number of analysts who went on to do great things. One of the most memorable was a young man named Rodney White. After graduating from Syracuse University in 1951, Rodney studied at Yale Law School but dropped out to join the Navy. After scoring highest on a qualifying exam for the Navy legal justice school, he instead chose to become a hard-hat diver and expert in underwater demolition. After five years in the Navy, he attended the Wharton School of Business at the University of Pennsylvania, where he helped pay for his education by playing jazz piano at night. Rod was also a terrific athlete and, according to a succession of moonstruck women, a great dancer.

The combination of jazz pianist, dancer, and underwater demolition expert was exactly what I was looking for in an analyst, and so I hired Rodney shortly after meeting him. He had called me from Halle & Steiglitz, where he then worked, seeking information about Woolworth, a stock we both followed. I turned the tables and began asking him questions. It turned out that he was not very happy in his job, and it was not difficult to lure him away. Rodney possessed one of the most able financial minds I have ever encountered, and he was a key figure in the firm's growth, pushing us into institutional sales, until he died in an accident in 1969.

In the late 1950s, I met a young man named Sanford Bernstein, who was then working as assistant to the chairman of the grocery chain Food Fair. An acquaintance who managed the pension fund for the Bulova Watch Company told me that Bernstein was an extremely able man. He also was loud and profane (at least in those early days before he moved to Israel, became devout, and ended up buried on the Mount of Olives). He worked in a T-shirt and summoned his secretary by sounding one of those loud Klaxon horns used on London taxis. He immediately grated on Rodney's nerves. (Ultimately, he left Oppenheimer and founded his own firm, Sanford C. Bernstein and Co., luring a number of Oppenheimer employees to join him when he did so. He might have been difficult, but the promise of money and position seemed to overcome personal feelings. One of these talented employees was Roger Hertog, a former student of mine when I taught securities analysis at City College. Roger later became president of Sanford C. Bernstein and Co.)

Not content to have two larger-than-life egos at each other's throats, I had also hired Eugene Fenton, who was then at Neuberger Berman and had just received his master's degree in business from NYU. Fenton immediately irritated both Sandy and Rodney (and everybody else, for that matter). Gene was monomaniacally interested in money and constantly undercutting himself by his own avarice.

Nevertheless, Gene Fenton was brilliant. Next to my father, Gene probably had as much influence on my thinking about the nature of markets as anyone. He viewed the market as a football game in which there were 22 players on the field and 80,000 in the stands. Although only the players on the field were moving, everyone had a stake in what they did. Moreover, the action on the field affected the mood in the stands, and the mood in the stands affected the action on the field.

Fenton laid out his ideas in his master's thesis—probably one of the few master's theses in history that could be used by investors.

Fenton saw a cycle to markets that ran through five phases: accumulation, appreciation, exhaustion, distribution, and liquidation. He analyzed the interplay of ten factors—such as leading indicators, Fed policy on interest rates, credit expansion and contraction, institutional and individual investors—and the role they played in each phase.

Fenton was interested in the psychology of markets. Such thinking was highly unusual for that time. In particular, he looked at the perversely counterintuitive role of the mood of market observers. Put simply, at major turning points in markets, market prognosticators are generally wrong. Times of universal pessimism usually represent remarkable buying opportunities, and times of buoyant optimism are often a clarion call to sell.

The simple reason, now well known and endlessly repeated in the press, is that in times of universal optimism, most potential buyers of stock are already in the market, whereas in times of deep pessimism, investors are out of stocks, or are trying to get out. This doesn't mean that the professionals are always wrong, but if they are right for a protracted period, they have convinced their followers to invest or sell, and thus must be wrong in the end.

I was intrigued by Fenton's thinking. As I pondered this paradox, I could identify a psychological mechanism that brings about a market turn. For example, declining stock prices can ultimately cause people to panic and sell. But the moment they join the panic and sell stock, they also relieve the cause of their fears and become potential buyers. The act of selling removes the anxiety, restores equanimity, and gives them the cash to buy.

It sounds simple, but as anyone who has invested knows, moods are powerful, and it is not so easy to buy in a period of profound pessimism, even if your mind tells you a particular moment could be the buying opportunity of the decade. For one thing, all your friends are doing the opposite, For another, pessimism is based on plausible arguments. Although you might tell yourself the bottom is at hand, you can never know that for a fact. Playing the market is not a science, and the market is not characterized by causal relationships. In the midst of a panic, you might tell yourself that it is highly unlikely for the market to fall further, but you can never say it is inconceivable. However tiny, this room for doubt is wide enough to permit fears to flow in and paralyze the investor.

In the early 1960s Charles Brunie, an auto industry analyst, joined us as a partner. At 6-foot-5, Brunie was a physically imposing man, and a devoted Ayn Rand follower. He also had a first-class mind and a photographic memory for facts and numbers. He figured out a correlation between demand for new autos and scrappage rates that often gave him better insight into the direction of the industry than auto executives themselves had. He later became an excellent airline analyst as well.

No accounting of the talent at Oppenheimer would be complete without mention of Captain Horatio Oppenheimer, whose portrait still sits in my office. Early on, I decided that Oppenheimer needed a dour and respectable senior partner, but we did not want to spend much money on him. One day I came upon the perfect candidate in the form of a portrait of a nineteenth-century sea captain. In the portrait, the officer is seated and holding an octant, looking very much like a man who knows his way. The image is only slightly belied by his vaguely alarmed expression, but I thought this perfectly appropriate given the goings-on he would be surveying from his perch on my office wall.

I purchased the portrait and commissioned a small copper plaque for the bottom of the frame that reads *Captain Horatio Oppenheimer: 1775–1842*. On occasion, I have invoked this distinguished presence when I wanted to decline an offer to participate in a deal. Gazing up at our wise founder, I would say, "I don't think the captain would have wanted us to be in this deal."

Perhaps the most astute financial mind in the Oppenheimer galaxy was Daniel J. Bernstein. He was a customer of the firm, not an employee, but he maintained an office with us. His gift to the company was his willingness to discuss his thinking. He gave us insights into the mind of a master investor, providing daily lessons in how a good analyst thinks. My brother Jay (who even then devoted his time to developing the economic tools first proposed by my father as a way of predicting the course of an economy) used to have lunch weekly with Bernstein, Gene Fenton, Fred Stein, me, and a couple of others. Jay said that if he could adequately answer Bernstein's and Fenton's questions on an issue, then he could defend his position against anyone.

I met Danny Bernstein through Wally Scheuer, son of the legendary Sy Scheuer. Danny's father earned hundreds of thousands of dollars a year as an executive of Loews during the Depression, and Wally Scheuer recalls that when someone asked him why, with so many people out of work, he did not take a pay cut to $250,000 per year, the elder Bernstein replied, "Because then I would be known as a $250,000-a-year man."

Danny spent his time investing his inheritance profitably and giving away a good part of his profits to various left-wing causes. His philanthropy surfaced in the press on one occasion when he was accused of sending money to groups in South Africa that advocated armed resistance to the apartheid regime. But although he was generous with causes, Danny was cheap in the extreme. He was notorious among his friends for asking waiters to bring a pack of cigarettes and then buying only one. Wally Scheuer recalls that after he had paid for about twenty lunches in succession, Danny said, "Wally, you always pay for lunch; this time let's split it."

Danny's masterpiece of stinginess came after one of those lunches. After the meal, he and Wally planned to drive to Scarsdale together. Danny had parked his car on the street to avoid paying for a lot, and he was enraged to find a parking ticket on his car window. That was only the beginning. Once they were on the road, Wally glanced at the gas gauge and pointed out in alarm that it read empty. Danny refused to stop, however, because he disliked paying the extra gas taxes in the city. Sure enough, the car sputtered to a halt on the FDR Drive. Wally took the wheel and managed to get the car to a gas station. Aghast at the prices, however, Danny bought only enough to get them to his beloved gas station in Westchester.

Yet Danny was a bleeding heart who could be totally irrational—when grasshoppers infested his lawn in Scarsdale, he faced a moral quandary. Rather than kill the insects with pesticide, he had his book-keeper vacuum them up and release them far away.

Danny was smart, smart enough to sell short in a bull market and still make money. He was one of the first analysts I knew to realize that certain numbers have a mystique in the stock market. Once a stock rises above $10 a share, he argued, it had a better chance to continue rising than if it remained below $10. This principle has nothing to do with the number, of course, but everything to do with psychology. Prices above $10 seem to reassure investors about the stability of the stock and the solidity of the company. Many institutions have rules prohibiting them from buying stocks below $10, the premise being that stocks selling below $10 are highly speculative. We know today that the price of the stock has nothing to do with the fundamental business or its risk, but somehow in the minds of investors, $10 was chosen as the arbitrary figure for stability.

One of Danny Bernstein's great plays was American Motors Company. Evaluating Volkswagen's success in the 1950s, he reasoned that there was a market for a small American car. With typical diligence, he began analyzing the company and watching the reports for ten-day auto sales. The company was doing well, and he began accumulating stock at around $5 a share. He also sought and obtained a meeting with George Romney, then the chairman of American Motors and later governor of Michigan. Romney was impressed with Danny's probing questions. He probably assumed that the New Yorker, in his cheap suit and unshined shoes, was badly in need of a job, and he suggested that Danny meet with the company's director of marketing. When Danny, whose stock was in the name of his broker, quietly informed Romney that he owned more shares of American Motors than Romney did, the chairman was flabbergasted.

Eventually, AMC peaked at over $100 a share (another significant number, according to Danny). Ultimately, though, its success proved its undoing. As a stock rises, corporate executives try to find savings and sales growth every way they can to increase earnings and justify the stock price. One fatal mistake many companies make is to cut back on quality and service. Over time, that begins to produce complaints, and Danny, ever the tireless observer of his investments, bailed out of AMC when he detected a decline in quality. Because I believed implicitly in his analysis, I went into AMC stock when Danny did and got out with a good profit.

Daniel Bernstein died of leukemia at age 51 in 1970. He left behind a legacy of good works that reflected his diligence and originality. He started the National Scholarship Fund and Service for Negro Students when, after calling around the country, he realized there were many scholarships for African Americans that went begging simply because students weren't aware of them. He was able to enlist scores of college presidents to support the effort. Also a vocal opponent of the war in Vietnam, he paid for a series of ads in *The New York Times* that listed the names of professors and other prominent Americans who called for an end to American involvement.

Although Danny was clearly a master of the game, making money was not an end in itself for him. I think that is true of many successful people in finance. Apart from giving money away, they have passionate outside interests. George Soros wants to rescue civil society; Jim Wolfensohn, a gifted dealmaker who is now president of the World Bank, has a passion for music; Jon Corzine seamlessly stepped from running Goldman Sachs to pursuing a liberal agenda in the U.S. Senate.

It is easy to dismiss the outside indulgences of the rich as hobbies they can afford, but I think this misses the point. Quite often those outside interests provide an anchor or larger perspective that was essential to their success in finance. In the top financial ranks are disproportionate numbers of contrarians. (This makes perfect sense, since investors too deeply wedded to conventional wisdom will perform only as well as the bulk of the crowd.) These successful contrarians often have a worldview of which finance and the markets are but a small part.

Although I like the game as much as any of these players, my many outside interests not only help me keep the game in perspective, but I think also make me a better player in both general and specific ways. I founded the Levy Economics Institute of Bard College to explore the social impact of economic policy, but I have also greatly benefited from the academic work done there. Even my interest in ancient art has provided me with historical analogies that help put current events into perspective.

Still, it is very easy to get swept up in finance, and when I do, philanthropy is there to help remind me of life beyond the markets. In this sense, philanthropy has been an important motif of my career, not something I've turned to once I made money.

My involvement in philanthropy started in the early 1950s, during the McCarthy era. I was angered when I read about university professors who were fired simply for expressing views that were not in accord with the paranoid temper of the times. I transformed my anger into something constructive by establishing the Fund for Academic Freedom, which was administered by the American Association of University Professors, whose leaders I had met through my old army boss, and friend, Ed Hutton. The fund's mission was to provide financial aid to professors who found themselves the target of witch hunts. I turned to two people I trusted to serve on the board. One was my brother Jay, the other Ed Hutton. Both still serve as trustees. My involvement in the protection of academic freedom has taken some ironic twists, however, as times have changed.

The AAUP started as a worthy defender of academic freedom. Over the years, the organization has evolved into a union to protect tenure. Tenure, which gives professors a defense against capricious administrators, also had worthy roots at the turn of the twentieth century, as champions of enlightenment sought to protect professors who taught evolution from attacks by creationists. Next to Supreme Court justices, tenured professors have the safest guarantee of lifetime employment, regardless of how their performance deteriorates.

Recently, I was forcefully reminded of the changed mission of the AAUP when the fates almost pitted one arm of my philanthropy against another. A distinguished academic institution to which I have given money had hired a professor for a tenured chair in one of the sciences. To the surprise of the administration, the man had promptly turned away from science and toward mysticism. This left the institution funding a vital and very expensive chair, but with nobody interested in science occupying it. The professor was offered a three-year grace period to find a new position more suited to his interests. He agreed to this arrangement, but after failing to find another job, he argued that the agreement was nonbinding. He further threatened to take his case to the AAUP. Fortunately, this never came to pass, or I might have found myself helping to fund both sides of the dispute.

5

A Fresh Look at the Familiar

MOST PEOPLE ARE extremely uncomfortable when investing in unconventional ways. Although economic theorists offer an idealized image of investors as rational beings who calmly assess opportunities, the typical investor I've met is idiosyncratic, superstitious, and, perhaps most important, prey to fears of the unknown. In short, he or she likes company. But the unconventional is what often creates opportunity. Investing probably is not played best as a group sport.

I had a dramatic encounter with this phenomenon in the early days of Oppenheimer, when we decided to go into the mutual fund business. Although mutual funds then were but a tiny fraction of the Goliaths that move trillions of dollars today, by the late 1950s, such managed investments were already perceived to be a mature business. It was a very staid field, run largely by Boston-based firms such as Fidelity, Putnam, State Street, and Mass Mutual. Dealmakers and investment bankers scorned mutual funds, but I saw wonderful opportunities for Oppenheimer. The inherent conflict of interest between a broker's desire to earn commissions and his responsibility to protect his customers' financial well-being largely disappeared with a mutual fund. And because a fund manager's salary depended on performance, this arrangement eliminated the major conflict with clients. When a broker left for another firm, he often took his customers with him, but if the customer had invested in a mutual fund, the managing company was much less vulnerable to such defections.

The management company grew as money came in, but it also collected a fee that was a percentage of assets. Consequently, a mutual fund grew in lockstep with the market. It grew while we slept and while we were on vacation, so long as our performance attracted customers.

As a child of the Depression, I knew very well that markets could fall. Even in the late 1950s, I still worried that the economy might slide back into a depression. Despite my predilection for hiring younger analysts with no memories of the crash, I had plenty of memories of the crash.

This tendency to look over my shoulder manifested itself in the criteria I stressed if we were going to enter the mutual fund business. To protect the fund in a down market, it had to be able to sell stocks short, because I was mindful that stock prices can be overvalued as well as undervalued. Everybody else on Wall Street knew this too, but no mutual fund that sold shares to the public had ever sought permission to sell short, as far as I knew. The fund also had to be able to take large enough positions to gain control of companies should stocks get so cheap that they were selling below the value of the underlying businesses. To a degree, this approach grew out of my fondness for special situations and my appreciation of the great rewards reaped by Sy Scheuer and other active investors.

Whereas much of Wall Street analyzed funds in terms of their track record, this view was based not on tradition but rather on what a mutual fund should be able to do to survive on the defensive as well as on the offensive. All of these innovations were prudent and conservative, because they were geared to protecting capital. Thus, I was taken aback when, once the Oppenheimer Fund was launched, the press criticized this approach as speculative. In retrospect, we should not have been surprised. Our mistake in launching the Oppenheimer Fund was in not sufficiently appreciating how skepticism about the unfamiliar can obscure the merits of even the best ideas.

I was taking a different look at the familiar and assuming that others would see the world the way I saw it. Rather than adhering to conventional wisdom on what mutual funds could or could not do, I looked at the virtues of their structure and then thought, wouldn't it be great if a mutual fund could operate like a successful investor. All of the innovations were familiar to any financier, but no one had previously tried to use them in a mutual fund.

The Oppenheimer Funds, which today have about $120 billion in assets, began with a chance encounter at a lower Fifth Avenue cocktail party in 1957 at the apartment of Edgar John Davies, who worked in Oppenheimer's corporate finance department. There were a number of Oppenheimer people there, including my secretary, Marni Cone. Marni knew I had been toying with the idea of starting a mutual fund in which the management fee was based on performance and not on the fund's assets. This fee arrangement seemed fair, since the fund manager's rewards were determined by what the fund delivered to investors. (When taking a flight, you want the pilot on the plane for the ride.) During the party, Marni pointed out a young man to me. "See that man over there," she said with the satisfaction of someone who knows she is delivering highly interesting news. "He just set up a fund with a performance fee."

I immediately asked to meet him, and Marni introduced me to Edmund Delaney, then a senior partner at the law firm of Palmer, Serles, Delaney, Shaw & Pomeroy. He was a cultured man whose courtly manner took the edge off his skills as an insistent and persuasive debater. I warmed to him immediately. He said that indeed he had set up a fund in which the managers were paid based on the fund's performance. "You can't do that," I protested. He countered, "We just did." It was the Leon B. Allen Fund.

Delaney had a rich life beyond his occupation in the law. He was an amateur historian who published several books, including works on Turtle Bay, Greenwich Village, and the Connecticut River. We agreed to have lunch, and I laid out the other innovations I wanted Oppenheimer's new mutual fund to embody. It took over two years of argument by Delaney, me, and others to convince the SEC to let the fund sell short.

We would travel down to Washington and lobby Eugene Rotberg at the SEC as well as Emanuel Cohen, who was then the chairman. After we persuaded Cohen to agree on an appropriate performance fee for the fund, I suggested we make a joint announcement. Cohen flung himself onto the couch in his office in mock exasperation and said, "You mean, Leon, that you want the SEC to advertise the Oppenheimer Fund." We launched the Oppenheimer Fund in 1959. Although we didn't call it a mutual hedge fund, it was the first such fund approved by the SEC that was open to small investors.

Any sense of satisfaction at this accomplishment was deflated when, not long after we launched the fund, an article appeared in *Fortune* magazine dismissing it as speculative, precisely because it could sell short. What I saw as prudent, the establishment viewed as radical. We realized then that we could not market the fund as conservative. Furthermore, the stigma of short selling caused us trouble when we went about registering the fund in different states, each of which had its own regulations.

I should have realized that although my memories of the Depression logically pointed me toward short selling as a hedge, in other minds, short selling was one of the bitter memories of the Depression. For all the work we put into getting approval to sell short (and for all the public relations problems this caused us), we could have saved ourselves a lot of trouble, because the fund never did much short selling in the end.

We did, however, more vigorously pursue some of my other innovations, although in one instance, we had a problem with appearances. In this case, however, the problem was internal rather than in the marketplace.

The venture in question was a uranium mine. To me, it looked like a great opportunity for profit with low risks. To Max, it looked like an unsavory fly-by-night speculation that would besmirch the Oppenheimer Fund name. In the late 1950s, many investors were smarting from losses inflicted by the collapse of an earlier speculative frenzy in uranium. Much of the activity in uranium was in penny stocks traded on the Salt Lake City exchange. When I wanted to buy the preferred stock of Hidden Splendor Mines for about 85 cents a share, Max objected, asking how it would look for the newly formed Oppenheimer Fund to own a stock that cost less than a dollar (another example of the mystique of numbers). I responded that nobody would care what a stock initially cost if it helped put Oppenheimer ahead of the pack in performance over the next five years. My reasons for looking at Hidden Splendor were conservative rather than speculative.

The uranium bubble serves as a reminder of how an infatuation with new technologies can eclipse the reasoning ability of the most sober investors. This bubble, a minor star compared with the supernova of the Internet bubble, grew from America's short-lived love affair with the nuclear age. In 1953 and 1954, foreseeing vast demand for uranium to provide the fuel to generate electricity, power motors, and blow us all to kingdom come, some Americans threw over their careers to become prospectors. Others played the Salt Lake City markets, where at the height of the frenzy, some stocks soared five-fold in a day. The bubble burst, as all bubbles do, when investors soured on empty and inflated claims and illusory profits. But, as often happens, in the rush to the exits, investors forgot about the special circumstances that made uranium appealing in the first place.

One such circumstance was that the U.S. Defense Mineral Exploration Administration (DMEA) regarded uranium as a strategic resource and guaranteed payment for pure yellowcake at $8 per pound. Thus, a uranium mine owner did not have to worry about oversupply driving down price, which temporarily removed a key element of risk. Moreover, the government would lend 75 percent of the money for uranium exploration through the program, and if the mine turned up empty, the DMEA would forgive repayment of the loan, removing another element of risk. Finally, I was able to reduce one other risk factor—the liars and charlatans who prowled the uranium markets—by finding what seemed to be the one honorable broker in the whole business. This was Payne Kibbe, a Salt Lake–based uranium specialist I met when I invested in a stock called Lisbon Uranium. He was a broker who offered to sell or buy shares of the company.

Oppenheimer and Company formed a private uranium company, Hilary Minerals, named after the oldest daughter of Joe Kanter, our uranium company partner. We started advertising for claims and looking for opportunities in the traded stocks of existing mines. Among other things, this led us to Hidden Splendor, a publicly traded stock that we bought for the Oppenheimer Fund.

The mine eventually ended up under the control of Atlas Corporation, an investment firm managed by Floyd Odlum, a uranium mogul. Odlum was a bold figure who had married aviatrix Jacqueline Cochran and had made several fortunes. During the Depression, he bought investment trusts at discounted prices and sold the underlying companies. Once Odlum decided that nuclear energy was the power supply of the future, he began acquiring claims and mines and made his Atlas Corporation the country's largest uranium-mining conglomerate.

Hidden Splendor had a diminishing supply of stock and an almost assured income through the government's program to buy uranium. The mine's preferred stock was being retired through a 20 percent annual sinking fund. After five years, there would be no preferred stock left, and we would be bought out at a higher price than we had paid to get in. This investment paid off, for both the Oppenheimer Fund and me, but overall, uranium proved to be a disappointment.

I enjoyed treking around out West with hard-rock geologists. For someone coming from a world in which three years is an eternity, it was interesting to encounter the perspective of scientists who could envision and reconstruct the slow unfolding of events over hundreds of millions of years. Payne Kibbe went on to become president of Lisbon Uranium and then to succeed Floyd Odlum as the head of Atlas Corporation and as president of Hidden Splendor.

Oppenheimer and Company also bought into a silver mine on the Utah–Nevada border. I visited the warren of tunnels, donning a miner's hat and descending into the gloom. It was like a subway with no lights. After the mine yielded a decent amount of ore, we lost sight of the vein and never found it again. Ultimately, we had to abandon the mine.

We had better luck with oil, chiefly through our association with Richard Lowe. An ingenious wildcatter (who among other things discovered an oil-rich fault that ran from the western states up into Canada), Lowe had a suspicion that if he pumped enough water from a well in certain locations, he would eventually hit oil. It was almost always the other way around, but damned if he wasn't right. With his partners, Lowe formed American Quasar, which was, in effect, a mutual fund for oil. We sold our oil companies to Quasar in exchange for stock, and I was given a position on the board. Evidently, I asked too many questions, and in time I was asked to resign. As it happened, this was a generous gesture on their part, since it freed me to sell the vastly overvalued stock. Dick Lowe could not sell, however (because he was an insider), and sadly, he went broke, though he managed eventually to recoup.

The early years of the Oppenheimer Fund gave me a crash course in the panoply of ways the psychology of investors and money managers intrude on markets. Fear of the unknown blinded people to opportunities; unpleasant memories of past markets caused the public to see essentially conservative strategies as speculative and somehow unsavory. At one point, we adopted a selling line that we viewed as bold, promising to invest anywhere in the free world where opportunity exceeded risk, only to discover that this promise scared, rather than attracted, potential customers.

The experience opened our eyes to the power of perception. We began to research the attitude of potential customers toward investments. To help us market and sell the funds, we hired Donald Spiro from the Dreyfus Fund, paying indirect homage to Jack Dreyfus who, more than anyone else, understood the power of psychology in selling mutual funds and was the most farsighted strategist in the field. He was among the first to advertise on television—indeed, Dreyfus was the second client of the pioneering advertising agency Doyle Dane & Bernbach. The Dreyfus symbol of a lion emerging from a subway struck a responsive chord with the public.

Spiro had been hired by Dreyfus explicitly because he had no experience in the securities industry. Jack Dreyfus's logic was that to

sell mutual funds, you needed to view them as an outsider would—
which was my thinking when I first considered starting a mutual
fund. This orientation is not as easy as it sounds. Trying to take a
similar approach, we hired a small advertising agency called Gordon
and Weiss and asked the firm to develop a symbol for the Oppenheimer Fund. The agency's first effort showed a discus thrower, an
idea I had originally suggested. Under withering fire from my partners, and confronted with devastating market research (something
about flinging an object off into space did not comfort investors), I
withdrew my suggestion, and we sent the ad men back to the drawing table.

Fortunately, we had on the Oppenheimer Fund board a mathe-
matician named Benjamin Lipstein who was an expert in market
testing of public attitudes. He was then the head of market research
at the advertising firm of SSC&B. Lipstein suggested that instead of
developing symbols and testing them on an audience, we try to
determine what customers looked for in a mutual fund and then
come up with the symbol.

With that in mind, we recast our research and discovered that the
desired qualities were strength, unity, a strong organization, single-
ness of purpose, and familiarity. It was obvious that we were failing
abjectly on this last point. With this new information, Gordon and
Weiss again went back to work, and some weeks later, we were
invited to see the possibilities the agency had come up with.

We entered a conference room to find perhaps 200 different symbols pasted to the walls. We went through the array one by one, taking down those we did not like, until we were down to three: a key, a
lighthouse, and four hands linked by grasping the wrists. This last
appealed to us because it suggested both individual strength and
cooperation and, perhaps most important, security. In that day, every
child knew about linking wrists to form a seat in order to carry

injured people away from a fire. Indeed, when we researched whether it was registered under copyright laws, we discovered that its first use in the United States was by Benjamin Franklin as a symbol that people posted by the street to alert private fire departments that the household was insured by his company. The symbol had never been registered, however, and we were free to use it.

Thus, we began marketing the Oppenheimer Fund for what it promised—financial security in retirement, payment for the kids' college education—because in those days, SEC regulations did not allow us to advertise our record. Even so, performance was the other key ingredient in our efforts to sell the fund, since past performance was a matter of record, and in the first years of the fund, performance was spectacular. This enabled us to deliver with confidence the simplest message of all: We will make your money grow.

Although the Oppenheimer Fund was never number one in any given year, over its first ten years, it had the best performance record of any mutual fund in the country, according to *The New York Times*. Our success attracted new investors, and the fund grew. We needed a ten-year record in order to have a strong story to sell to customers. This put us in a somewhat contradictory situation, however, since even as we were telling customers not to look at any given year but at our long-term record, we were motivating our managers by telling them that a ten-year growth record is nothing more than a succession of short-term performances strung together back to back.

This period of rapid growth was not without its setbacks. Stocks fell rapidly in 1962 when JFK tried to keep the lid on steel prices. Despite the fact that our fund managers thought the overall market would go down, they all believed that their favored stocks would buck the trend. They were wrong. In April 1962, the fund shrank in value from roughly $17 million to $13 million. In the summer, we concluded that the bear market was probably over and became somewhat more aggressive. The trend reversed, and our fund increased more than the rest of the market—we were probably in more volatile stocks—as we beefed up our performance.

The Cuban missile crisis was also a time when we had a major market setback. Max reacted with great alarm, suggesting that we move the company's files to storage in the Adirondacks to safeguard customer accounts in the event of a war. Hearing this ludicrously optimistic take on the aftermath of a nuclear attack, I thought we ought to be moving the partners to safe storage, not the files. Max told us to go on a "war footing" with our investments. We stayed in stocks and tried to stay cool.

When he wasn't worrying about the practical details of nuclear Armageddon, Max was nervously watching over the fund. He would walk up to Don Spiro, put an arm around his shoulders (at six feet, four inches, Max towered over most of us), and say in his thick German accent, "These are good stories you have, but vere are the orders?"

Apart from performance, a key element in the success of the fund was the sales force. Psychology played a role here as well. In the mid-1960s, I read an article in the *Harvard Business Review* about a Princeton-based psychologist named Herbert Greenberg, who claimed he could predict a salesman's ability through a psychological exam that probed traits such as ego, empathy, and the ability to get along with other people. I invited him to our offices. (Observant fellow that I am, I never noticed he was blind until an associate pointed it out to me after he left). All the partners took the test under pseudonyms. Mine was Art Loft, and the results suggested that I had top potential as a salesman but limited ability as a manager. Among the more trenchant observations about me in the report was this: "He is quite impulsive, does not tolerate detail too well."

Since the test nailed each of our personalities, we adopted it as one of the ways we predicted the probable success of future recruits. Oppenheimer and Company still uses the test today, and Don Spiro gives a lot of credit to Dr. Greenberg's test for helping him build up our marketing ability.

As Oppenheimer and Company prospered, my old firm Hirsch and Company headed in the other direction. If one of our firm's early problems was inattention to public perception in pursuit of performance, Hirsch regularly sacrificed performance in pursuit of appearances. Its last move along these lines proved fatal when it agreed to merge with the staid and well-established firm of Francis I. Dupont & Co. in 1970. It was precisely the wrong time for Hirsch to be linking its fate with a firm that depended on fixed commissions and the old-boy network. As the economy grew, it became obvious that competition would increase and large institutions would demand an end to fixed rates. These conditions ultimately spawned the discount brokers for individuals.

Trading volume soared, precipitating major changes in the way in which stocks were sold and who sold them. The WASP firms began opening their doors to Catholics and Jews, and the Jewish firms started attracting WASPs. Oppenheimer initially was an entirely Jewish firm, but as times changed, so did we; after all, we simply wanted to be successful. By 1970 there were several non-Jewish partners. Among them were Charles Brunie, our auto industry analyst; Jimmy King, whose family came from China; Don Spiro, our key marketing person for the Oppenheimer Funds; and Powell Cabot, whose ancestors made their fortune with the Hudson Bay Company trading beaver pelts with Indian tribes in the far north.

Once, at a dinner at Powell Cabot's house in London, the subject of ancestry came up—in his home he had a portrait of one of his ancestors, a founder of the British firm Kleinwort Benson. Powell, who was very diffident about his famous name, remarked in a self-deprecating way that someone had traced his ancestry back several hundred years. Knowing that the West can't hold a candle to the East in this regard, I remarked to Jimmy King, who was sitting next to me, "Can't you trace yours back 2,000 years?" Without missing a beat, Jimmy replied, "Yes, but the first 200 years were probably apocryphal." He was joking but also being accurate, since an ancient Chinese dynasty was toppled by an invasion from the south in about 300 A.D., and the more prosperous Chinese busily rewrote their ancestry to avoid disfavor with the new power structure. The Levy line, of course, goes back into the mists of time—as does everybody's. I'm fond of the lyric in Gilbert and Sullivan's *Mikado* in which Poobah declaims that he can trace his ancestry back to a primordial particle.

The clubby, sleepy world of fixed commissions gave way to negotiated fees, as block trading shifted power from those trading the stocks to institutions that could dangle the promise of huge block trades and thus shop around for the best prices. Block trading was tempting, because it offered a company power in the marketplace, but it was a double-edged sword, since negotiated fees meant lower commissions. Still, if a firm wanted to expand its institutional business, it had to offer block trades along with research, since institutions now demanded more liquidity. At this critical time of transition for the firm, it was Jack Nash who provided the leadership to keep the firm growing. He brought in Willie Weinstein, a family friend whom he knew and trusted, to run our block trading operation. Without a block trading department, Oppenheimer would have remained a research boutique and been swallowed up by a larger firm, the eventual fate of most such boutiques.

As trades got larger, firms needed more capital, and this rapid demand for large amounts of new money forced profound changes on financial firms. In 1970, I had a chat with John L. Loeb about the stresses of growing firms. Loeb was a Wall Street legend, who founded Loeb Rhoades and Company with family money. We were sitting together at a lunch at Bankers Trust and talking about Donaldson, Lufkin, and Jenrette, which had broken with tradition by going public—the first Wall Street firm to do so. Loeb was appalled; he did not think firms should be able to solicit outside capital. I asked him what he did when his firm needed extra money. He replied, "Why, we simply call one of our aunts." At that time, firms could accept subordinated loans only from relatives; since Loeb was related to some of New York's wealthiest banking families, that was easy for him.

"What do you do," I asked, "if you don't have an aunt?" He never answered my follow-up question, because he had already ruled out the one obvious answer: Go public.

Some people questioned the correctness of a company going public when its only assets rode the elevators (a criticism also leveled at advertising agencies, which started going public around that time), but the changes on Wall Street permitted financiers to keep pace with rapidly expanding institutional trading. Without the introduction of competition and new sources of capital, it is unclear whether New York would have displaced London as the financial capital of the world in the early 1970s.

Oppenheimer did not go public. We remained a partnership because we had an investment account that in good years gave us large profits, and a partnership structure had tax advantages over a public company. We also preferred the flexibility of being private. We could change structure any time we wanted without going through the elaborate rigamarole required of a public company.

We preferred to answer to as few people as possible—and all the better if those few investors were sophisticated and imaginative as well. The price of this freedom, however, was the periodic liquidity crunch. When we needed capital, we couldn't sell shares; instead we invited limited partners to invest or obtained subordinated loans from private equity trusts. Unfortunately, the facts of life are that cash is readily available when you don't need it, and not available when you do. Jack Nash observed that during good times, everybody wants to be a partner, but during bad times, everybody wants to be a vice president.

The 1960s proved to be a crucial transitional decade as investment banks and brokerage houses adapted to growth, competition, and other forces. By focusing on investment performance, Oppenheimer and Company found itself well positioned to profit as Wall Street was swept by change. Hirsch bet on the old world and sank from view, along with Francis I. Dupont, its new partner.

6

Beware Overreachers

IN THE SPRING AND SUMMER OF 2002, the U.S. financial markets endured their own version of the Reign of Terror that followed the French Revolution. The aristocrats of the markets of the 1990s were dragged before the authorities to be stripped of their jobs and humiliated before a public demanding blood for the trillions of dollars lost and hundreds of thousands of jobs that disappeared as a result of a declining economy, exacerbated by accounting scandals, analyst hoodwinking, and other financial sins. Many of these "evil-doers" (to borrow a phrase from George W. Bush) started out honestly, but as their companies grew, the markets demanded ever more growth, and they all discovered a fundamental truth: Sustaining performance over time is very, very hard.

Faced with a choice of disappointing their shareholders or their conscience, many made the same choice: They cheated. The scale of corruption uncovered in America's balance sheets and investment banks has been impressive, but the overreachers who cooked the books are hardy perennials that pop up whenever opportunity presents itself during the long march of financial folly. Overreachers are an endemic part of the financial landscape—they are like weeds in summer. I've encountered many overreachers in my career. The trick is to recognize early on both their brilliance and their fatal flaws.

Markets offer the biggest opportunity for rewards to those who are willing to take the most risk. You might ignore an opportunity to earn 0.3 percent on an investment, but if you can leverage your investment 100 times through borrowing, you can earn 30 percent on your capital. Of course, if you do this, you had better be right. For this reason, the market draws highly competitive people with an appetite for risk. Leverage may not change the odds of a given investment, but it makes the consequences much more stomach-turning if the investment turns bad and you end up with a pile of debt.

The market attracts a particularly aggressive breed of people and then puts them in situations where the very aggressiveness that fostered their success will sometimes hustle them off the stage. The market first rewards overreachers and then punishes them later.

My Oppenheimer colleague Gene Fenton was such an overreacher. As I saw from his innovative thinking on the nature of markets, Gene was brilliant and possessed all the qualities that should have made him a highly successful investor—but his weaknesses ultimately negated many of his good qualities. He was a misanthropic, driven man, completely focused on money and markets. Gene's overreaching was so interesting because he was aware of it. As a student of markets and psychology, he was mindful of the fatal chemistry of human nature and markets.

Unfortunately, he couldn't help himself. Gene was extremely difficult to work with. His secretaries were constantly quitting or being fired, and it was hard for him to work with others. He, too, got restless, and in the early 1960s began plotting his exit. His idea was to move to California and buy a savings and loan. (He also thought the California way of life would be more to his liking—golf in summer and skiing in winter.) He would use the S&L as a vehicle to make his fortune, then he would give up his U.S. citizenship—Gene hated paying taxes—and move to the Caribbean. I pointed out to him that on many islands, the natives did not care much for whites given the sorry history of the races. He replied that he understood that perfectly, and that he didn't much like whites either.

As with much of Gene's logic, there was a core of astute analysis in his cockamamie scheme. Most aggressive investors at that time shunned S&Ls because they were restricted to lending for mortgages, and they were always in peril of insolvency because they had to pay highly variable short-term rates to attract depositors. If short-term rates suddenly rose, the S&Ls could be stuck with high costs of money while their income remained limited by the return on long-term mortgages. One great investment maxim is pertinent here: Never borrow short term against long-term debt, and beware of the stocks of companies that do.

In 1957, Lehman Brothers introduced the first public savings and loan, Great Western Financial. This opened Gene's eyes to the possibilities of tapping into the S&Ls' accumulated earnings, which previously had been held as reserves against bad debts. Earnings of S&Ls went into a general reserve fund that was not taxable, but not available for dividends either. This created the possibility of shifting some of these retained earnings to a taxable earned surplus that could be paid out as dividends. Moreover, S&Ls seemed to hold the promise of being a type of perpetual-motion machine. By offering higher interest rates, an S&L could attract virtually unlimited amounts of money.

The problem was the classic bind of borrowing short and lending long. If short-term rates rose rapidly, a bank would find itself hemorrhaging money, because its cost to borrow money would rise while its income from long-term loans and mortgages remained fixed. Gene had a solution to that, and it was brilliant. Its one flaw derived directly from Gene's Achilles heel—overreaching.

The idea was the variable-rate mortgage (now universally known as the adjustable-rate mortgage). A mortgage that allowed the lender to adjust rates on mortgages as short-term interest rates fluctuated would protect the S&L from being caught in an interest rate squeeze. It was a brilliant idea that Gene got half right: In Gene's innovation, the variable rate of the mortgage would only go up. Despite this, I liked Gene's analysis of the promise of S&Ls, and when he solicited me as a potential investor, I agreed to become his partner. We considered the investment too risky for the firm, but several other partners also bought in.

In the early 1960s, Gene bought Contra Costa Savings and Loan in Concord, California, for $600,000, and we were in business. But I had a sense of dread. For one thing, Gene's abrasiveness and legendary cheapness were sure to get us in trouble. And it did. I recall vividly one occasion when we were driving to Sacramento to sort out some problem. We were scheduled to meet with Preston Martin, who was then California's commissioner of savings and loans. For the most part, S&L officials in California were little caesars, but Martin was a smart and highly capable man. As we motored toward the state capital, I noticed we were running low on gas. In classic Fenton style, Gene wanted to reach a discount gas station thirty miles ahead. Of course, we ran out of gas. It was vintage Fenton that he would jeopardize a meeting that could affect the fate of a large investment rather than spend a few cents more for gas. (Gene was cheap, but at least he was consistent. When he got married in California, he asked the saleslady if it was possible to rent a wedding dress because, he explained, his fiancée "would only be wearing it once.")

That episode served as a forceful reminder of the difficult and peculiar nature of my partner in this investment. Shortly after we bought our first S&L, Gene and I were driving through Marin County when he asked me what I worried about late at night. Without hesitation I replied that my nightmare was that he would call me and tell me "that Preston Martin had quit as commissioner, that our board wanted to resign, and that the new S&L commissioner was going to close us down." To varying degrees, all of these things happened.

For starters, the S&L commissioners viewed us as the bad guys. As newcomers who paid higher interest to lure deposits and explored innovations such as the variable-rate mortgage, we aroused their suspicions. We also incurred the wrath of the Federal Home Loan Bank Board, which passed judgment on whether a bank could open new branches. Had it not been for the open-minded Preston Martin, who was first a California commissioner and then head of the Home Loan Bank Board in Washington, our S&L venture might have been a complete disaster.

Although Martin allowed us to go forward, we were victimized by Gene's blindness. To his surprise, people did not storm the gates to apply for mortgages whose rates could only go up. Gene failed to see how to transform his brilliant insight into an idea that might have had traction in the marketplace. Had he taken the risk and allowed rates to go down as well as up, he might have become one of the richest men in America.

What Gene could not see, however, others could. Another Oppenheimer employee, Marion Sandler—whom Gene had recruited—studied Gene's mistakes and realized that the variable-rate mortgage had enormous potential in the marketplace if rates varied both up and down. The S&L might offer lower monthly payments than traditional fixed-rate mortgages. Marion left Oppenheimer, and with her husband, Herb (who happened to be my lawyer), took over a savings and loan that they subsequently named Golden West Financial. Drawing customers with adjustable-rate mortgages, Golden West ultimately became one of the largest S&Ls in the United States, and Marion Sandler became one of the most successful women in America.

Gene never fulfilled his dubious dream of renouncing his U.S. citizenship and thus avoiding taxes. Years later, he developed a virulent form of cancer and died suddenly in 1976. A dozen years after he died, however, much of the S&L industry succumbed to Gene's fatal flaws—greed and overreaching. Collusion between S&L lobbyists and Congress led to an ill-conceived deregulation of the S&L industry during the Reagan years that produced an orgy of self-dealing, looting, and dubious loans. Congress then papered over its mistake by authorizing a bailout that ultimately cost U.S. taxpayers $500 billion. (One of the few S&Ls to remain healthy was Golden West.) The bailout sum was but a fraction of the trillions lost in the post-1990s market meltdown, but still was a large amount of money. The S&L bailout did not spark the public outrage of today's crisis, possibly because most taxpayers were unaware that they picked up the tab for the greed and corruption of others.

Although Gene Fenton overreached, he stayed within the law. The same cannot be said about others I've encountered. Indeed, the number of people who at first make money legitimately but then descend the slippery slope to outright fraud offers a backhanded compliment to the relative efficiency of the markets over time. One man who crossed the line was Bernie Cornfeld. Cornfeld had an exotic biography. He was born in Istanbul (originally as Benno Cornfeld) and grew up in Brooklyn. A short, brilliant man with a stutter who nevertheless spoke five languages, he founded Investors Overseas Services (IOS) in 1956 as an offshore mutual fund sales company whose principal clients were GIs stationed in Europe. In 1962 he started The Fund of Funds, another offshore mutual fund whose mandate was to invest in the best mutual funds in the United States. The Fund of Funds was a good idea, but Cornfeld pushed it too far.

In the mid-1960s, Cornfeld's Fund of Funds bought $20 million worth of shares in the Oppenheimer Fund, making him our largest shareholder. We were wary of Cornfeld, and as a precaution, we made him sign a letter acknowledging that he could not tell us what stocks to put in the fund. Undeterred, Cornfeld made his bid a few years later to do exactly that. He sent Henry Buehl, one of his chief lieutenants, to us with the message that he wanted the Oppenheimer Fund to buy stock in a shoe company. I realized Cornfeld wanted to use us to prop up the company's stock price. I had anticipated this moment and showed Buehl the letter. We didn't buy the stock, and Cornfeld shortly thereafter sold his shares of the Oppenheimer Fund.

We could see then that Cornfeld was on an express train to the steel hotel. He was doing what Michael Milken tried years later with Drexel Burnham: giving inducements to those he invested with (or in Milken's case, raised junk financing) to in turn invest in his other deals. Cornfeld was also giving bonuses to his salesmen with IOS shares, a dilutive strategy that ultimately had to crash. The ploy was a giant chain letter or Ponzi scheme. The ironies compounded in 1971 when IOS, in the process of collapsing, was purchased by Robert Vesco, who was an even bigger crook than Cornfeld. Vesco went on to complete the looting of the fund and to perpetrate one of the biggest financial frauds of the time, before fleeing to Cuba and allegedly turning to drug smuggling.

Just before the IOS collapse, I had one other encounter with an overreacher from the Cornfeld solar system. This was John King, then a larger-than-life billionaire oil man who had built his fortune selling limited partnerships in oil exploration ventures. I'd agreed to this meeting at the urging of Arthur Lipper.

Lipper, a restless and creative intellect, had made his name by establishing performance measures for mutual funds (a business later acquired by his brother, Michael). Arthur hated doing anything that someone else was doing. He was always imagining new financial gambits—among them securitizing the S&P 500, an idea that was eventually developed by others. Among his far-flung ventures were an ice-skating rink in Singapore (which lies on the equator), vineyards in Australia, and a radio station that served the Gulf states on the Arabian peninsula (and whose most popular program was a reading of the Israeli casualty lists in the 1967 war, or so he told us). Lipper mentioned that King was looking for financing and urged me to visit the oil man in Denver.

I showed up at King's address and was ushered into an enormous office where this imposing giant sat beneath a portrait of a charging elephant—the image of a billionaire oil man right out of Central Casting. King laid out his proposition. He offered to sell me 20,000 acres of Arctic oil land, a small fraction of the 20 million acres held by King Arctic Investments, which in turn was largely held by Cornfeld's Fund of Funds. Moreover, if I agreed to the price of $8 per acre, King said I would not have to put up any money for eight years. Why would anyone want to sell a property and not receive money?

I had come armed with the answer. Shortly before visiting Denver, I had run into Louis Weeks, the retired chief geologist for Standard Oil. There are good geologists and great geologists, and Weeks certainly qualified as the latter. He combined scientific rigor and imagination. For years, Weeks presented one of the most popular programs on the Armed Forces Radio Network in Europe, in which he explained that modern geology confirmed the order of events in the Book of Genesis. Light into darkness, water onto land—that was exactly the sequence of events.

With his background, Weeks had superb instincts for the value of oil properties, and I asked him about the likely value of King's Arctic land. After some thought, he came back with the figure: about 50 cents per acre.

With that piece of information, I knew King and his buddy Bernie Cornfeld were in the last act of their financial drama. Had I purchased the acreage, King could have used that sale to mark up the value of his remaining millions of acres, and Cornfeld could maintain the illusion that the Arctic lands were still worth the $8 per acre that Cornfeld had paid for them, thus misleading the public as to the value of the assets in his Fund of Funds. When I called King to demur from the investment, I casually asked him whether he was worried about the SEC. With disarming candor, King replied, "No, I'm friendly with Richard Nixon, and he sent me the names of all candidates for chairman and asked me which ones I would not oppose."

Back in New York, I found my mind still spinning with the chance insight I had stumbled into concerning the unwinding of IOS and John King. That night I had dinner with Willie Morris, the editor of *Harper's Magazine*, and asked him if he would like me to write about the greatest financial story of the decade. He wasn't interested. Even so, King went to jail, while Cornfeld was held in a Swiss jail for eleven months before fraud charges were dropped. He died broke.

The financial markets attract their fair share of crooks, but some overreachers are brought down more by their ideals than their greed. Often these are people with energy and vision, and thus they are far more interesting than the merely greedy. Certainly, William Zeck-endorf fit this description; he left behind him a trail of bankrupt companies and irate investors but also monuments such as the United Nations building.

Zeckendorf was a rotund man with a red face that made him look as if he were a ripe tomato atop a huge watermelon. He kept an igloo-shaped office on Madison Avenue, next door to the office of the celebrated architect I. M. Pei, whom he had met through Nelson Rockefeller, the governor of New York. Although the public might benefit from the close propinquity of a developer and a great architect, a bit more distance — perhaps a floor — between the two would have been preferable. Here Zeckendorf reigned, surrounded by telephones like a great impresario, with his buildings as his stars. On the walls he kept photographs of the great buildings of the world, including the Parthenon.

Zeckendorf had two weaknesses: He wanted to build beautiful buildings, and he was addicted to doing deals. He was never as good at financial architecture as he was at building the real thing. Because of the risks of his projects and his checkered track record, the interest rates he had to pay were several points above the market rate, and it is arguable that no one can make money by continually paying sky high interest rates.

I first learned of Zeckendorf in 1957, when I heard he was planning to merge his wholly owned company Webb and Knapp with American Superpower, an investment company left over from the 1920s, in which he was the majority owner. I thought this might be an investment opportunity, and so I went down to Washington to listen in on the SEC's hearings on the proposed merger.

The only other observer at those hearings was Otto Hirshman, an interesting man who was then a partner at Dreyfus and Company and who described himself as a "stock market detective." A refugee from Holland, Hirshman had good instincts. It was Hirshman who later alerted me to some of the possibilities in uranium mining. In one conversation, Hirshman mentioned Roosevelt Field, a large property (in which Oppenheimer had a position) adjacent to an old airport on Long Island that Zeckendorf controlled through Webb and Knapp. Roosevelt Field had just bought from Webb and Knapp the McCreary department store, which had its main building on 33rd Street in Manhattan. Otto said, "Leon, you must find out whether Zeckendorf is shifting McCreary to Roosevelt Field in order to build up the shopping center, or just sticking a losing property onto the shareholders of Roosevelt Field."

Good question. We sent Frances Heidt to the Roosevelt Field annual meeting, and with some additional sleuthing, it became clear that Zeckendorf was offering the public shareholders of Roosevelt Field a chance to participate in losses that were previously his responsibility alone. I'm confident that Zeckendorf's motivation was not villainy or greed but rather a desperate maneuver to keep Webb and Knapp solvent. Nevertheless, it was a miserable way to treat the innocent and guileless shareholders of Roosevelt Field. So we sued.

We hired Milton Pollack, a brilliant lawyer who later became a distinguished federal judge. The suit unfolded slowly, and I fell into a ritual of having dinner with Pollack once a month during which he would update me on our progress and his methods. At that time he had a daughter in elementary school; he told me that before he asked any question of a witness, he would test it on his daughter.

Through disarming and deceptively simple questions, Pollack would gradually ensnare and then squeeze a witness. When it came time to depose Zeckendorf, this strategy worked brilliantly. At first charming and at ease, Zeckendorf began to perspire as Pollack quietly closed off every exit. In just one hour, Pollack got Zeckendorf to acknowledge that his motivation for shifting McCreary was to improve the books of Webb and Knapp at the expense of the share-holders of Roosevelt Field. Shortly thereafter, Zeckendorf settled the lawsuit.

Despite our differences, I admired Zeckendorf's single-minded zeal for constructing beautiful buildings. Years from now, his financial misadventures will be long forgotten, but he will be remembered as a developer with a soul. His willingness to pay (or have his investors pay) for beauty has improved the skylines of New York, Toronto, Denver, and every other city he touched. There was a grandeur to Zeckendorf's overreaching.

Ability and good character, sad to say, do not always appear together. And that is why overreachers will remain a part of the financial landscape no matter how moralistic and regulated we become in the aftermath of today's market meltdown. They think big and have the courage to explore the new.

7

Beauty and the Beast

AS INVESTORS, we deceive ourselves a thousand different ways, both small and large. We attribute gains to acumen when they are the product of luck, and attribute losses to ill fortune when they are often the product of stupidity or inattention. We believe that the market remembers or cares about the price we paid for a stock, or that our stocks will go up when every other stock is going down. But most commonly in markets, we fall in love with a company that is unworthy of our affection.

I've been left at the altar by more than one company. In particular, there were costly financial romances in which I was blinded by the charm of a company or its management. Disciplined investors must be able to see hidden beauty; conversely, they also must be able to look past the shimmer of some companies to see the rot within. In one investment in the 1960s, I got this exactly wrong. But when I got it right a decade later, against the backdrop of one of the most protracted bad markets in the post-Depression era, it more than made up for my earlier mistake.

Some of the best opportunities involve badly managed companies, if only because the situation can improve rapidly with the imposition of good management. No matter how bad a company, there is almost always a point where it is a bargain. This was the logic that led Oppenheimer in 1957 to take a position in Underwood, a miserably managed manufacturer of typewriters that was being trounced by IBM in the electric typewriter market. Olivetti bought a majority position in Underwood, and seduced by my admiration for Italian style and panache, I reasoned that the new Italian owners would turn Underwood around.

My impression was based on evidence. Olivetti was growing faster than IBM at that time. Olivetti made beautiful machines, treated its workers well, and was guided by dazzling and polished managers like Gianluigi Gabetti, who went on to lead IFI, the holding company for the family of the industrialist Gianni Agnelli. Ivrei, where Olivetti was headquartered, was a lovely Italian city dotted with buildings designed by some of the foremost architects of the day.

I figured that if a company does one thing well, it usually does many other things well. Consequently, I enthusiastically continued to buy Underwood stock to the point that the Oppenheimer Fund became its largest outside shareholder. Along with an investor named Ernest Oppenheimer (no relation to Max), we controlled about 20 percent of the stock.

We would have bought still more had I not been restrained by my colleague Archer Scherl, chief portfolio manager of the fund, who pointed out to me a minor detail: Underwood was losing money. I had suggested that the Oppenheimer Fund increase its position in the company, but he refused. We took the disagreement to the board, whose members heard both arguments but sided with Archer. In the end, the board's decision helped to insulate the fund somewhat from the events that followed.

Had nothing else changed, our investment might have worked out, but IBM had its own plans for the typewriter business. In 1961 it introduced a radically new concept for electric typewriters—the Selectric, which had all the characters on one ball that rotated and struck the paper. Though prone to breakdowns at first, the Selectric soon became a sensation in the electric typewriter market. Unable to respond to this technological juggernaut, Underwood went under and almost took Olivetti with it.

I did not always succumb to charm, however. Following the reports of insider stock transactions in 1962, I noticed that Nicholas Reisini, the CEO of Cinerama, was consistently buying his own stock. Figuring that he knew something, I bought a few shares and arranged to meet with him. He had a beautiful office on Park Avenue, furnished with antiques and attended to by beautiful secretaries. It was a Hollywood dream of an office, and he was a dynamic, charismatic CEO.

With no hesitancy, he told me his life history and then of his grand plans for Cinerama. He was planning to make films in three dimensions. He told me the plots of the movies he had under way, and each was more fascinating than the next. I was dazzled; that is, I was dazzled until I walked out of his elegant offices into a snowstorm and was suddenly struck with the thought that no one could be as good as I thought Reisini was. I resolved to sell the stock the day Cinerama's first movie, *How the West Was Won*, hit the screen. It was one of the few times I sold close to a stock's all-time high.

The mid-1970s were not a productive time for the markets, which stagnated between 1964 and 1982; the Dow closed at 874 in 1964 and at 875 in 1981, racking up a magnificent gain of one point in seventeen years. Anybody who began investing in the 1990s, and had the expectation that stocks regularly outperform all other investments, should spend a moment pondering those two numbers and two

dates. For example, say you were forty-eight years old in 1964 and put
$100,000 into the Dow on the last day of 1964 with instructions that
dividends be reinvested, confident that you would have a nice nest
egg when you retired at age sixty-five. When the last day of 1981
rolled around, your money would be worth statistically less than
your initial investment because of the moribund market and the
depredations of inflation.

During this time, Oppenheimer looked for investment opportunities outside the stock market. We challenged the broadcast license
of television station WPIX in New York, which was owned by the
Tribune Company, on behalf of a group of investors who wanted to
take over the station. We also gained control of the property company General Acceptance Corporation, which was the largest bankruptcy in Florida history. (The company is now known as Avatar.)
And we guided a financial services and oil company, CIC, through
its bankruptcy proceedings, enabling it to pay off its debts—at 100
cents on the dollar—and still have assets to sell.

The decline of 1974, when the Dow Jones Industrial Average fell
45 percent, put the final bullet into the so-called go-go years of the
stock market that began in the late 1960s. It was an era marked by
speculative manias over hi-tech and "gunslinger" money managers
who darted in and out of stocks and enjoyed celebrity status until the
Arab oil embargo ended the fun and games.

Every problem is an opportunity, however, and I began thinking
about the various forces at work in the market. One aspect of bad
markets caught my attention: Many companies carried divisions and
acquisitions on their books whose real value was in no way reflected
in the price of their shares. The late 1960s and early 1970s had been
a period of aggregation, as conglomerates such as ITT and Gulf +
Western formed and bought up companies, ostensibly to improve
synergies and efficiencies. These objectives proved mostly illusory,

and in the late 1970s, I began wondering whether the United States was about to enter a period of disaggregation, as frustrated executives began selling off the very properties they had spent so much energy acquiring just a few years earlier. If so, there was the opportunity for a broad-based arbitrage in realizing these values.

Then in 1977, a bitter winter brought about a shortage of natural gas and a second energy crisis, and the tumblers began to fall into place. On February 2, 1977, President Jimmy Carter appointed James Schlesinger as the nation's "energy czar" and charged him with finding ways to conserve energy and increase supplies. I attended one of Schlesinger's speeches in Washington in which he discussed turning to coal to make up for the shortfall in oil and natural gas supplies (this was before global-warming fears made coal environmental enemy number one).

I had some experience with the coal business from the 1950s as part of my efforts to decode the mysterious maneuverings of Sy Scheuer in his takeover of West Virginia Coal and Coke. I recalled that the real opportunity back then was not so much in mining the fossil fuel but in moving it. Our transportation analyst, Bert Fingerhut, had urged us to explore opportunities in railroads—one of the best ways of transporting large amounts of coal through great stretches of America. Thus I approached Schlesinger after his speech to ask him whether the United States had the railroad capacity to move the amounts of coal he was talking about. His answer, a qualified maybe, suggested that railroads were going to be operating at full capacity if his energy plan was enacted. This simple question led to one of the most interesting, complicated, and profitable investments of my career. It took years for this deal to come to fruition, but the bankruptcy of the Chicago, Milwaukee, St. Paul & Pacific Railroad presented a golden opportunity. Bankruptcies have often been extraordinarily profitable because they scare away many investors, which means their stock and bond prices are low.

I had been following railroads since the 1940s, when my father began buying the bonds of bankrupt railroad lines such as the Missouri Pacific and the Minneapolis, St. Paul & Sault Ste. Marie. Nearly half the nation's railroads went broke in the Depression. Mobilization for World War II briefly improved their situation, but railroads quickly fell on hard times again. This was in part because of the suffocating regulations of the Interstate Commerce Commission. Class One railroads could not merge without excruciatingly long hearings, nor could they abandon track. Where the ICC left off, the unions took over, forcing railroads to retain workers long after technology rendered their jobs obsolete.

By the mid-1970s, the ICC was well aware of this situation, and many of its commissioners regarded the rehabilitation of railroads almost as a patriotic duty. At one meeting I had in the late 1970s with an ICC commissioner, he noted that in Canada, railroad movement of freight had sped up during the twentieth century, whereas in the United States, it had slowed. Canada had coast-to-coast lines, but freight traversing the United States had to switch lines several times, with each switch causing delay and adding expense.

Bert Fingerhut and I flew to Washington to meet with various ICC commissioners. These conversations convinced us that the ICC was going to take dramatic steps to bolster American railroads. Our next task was to find a railroad that was going to benefit from these as yet unspecified changes.

To help us in this quest, we had hired Pat Cestaro, a former ICC lawyer. Large in girth and large in personality, Pat reminded me of Zero Mostel in the movie *The Producers*. He liked to play the wheeler-dealer role and sported flashy suspenders. Pat suggested that we take a hard look at the Chicago, Milwaukee, St. Paul & Pacific Railroad.

In most of the Wall Street community, his suggestion would have been greeted with a derisive snort, since in December 1977, the Milwaukee Road had just gone bankrupt for the third time. With oppressive regulations, aggressive unions, complicated accounting, and widely dispersed assets, railroads usually took many years to emerge from bankruptcy. The Milwaukee Road was losing $500,000 a day and had many thousands of miles of unprofitable and dilapidated track. Even its main trunk lines were so degraded that trains could travel no faster than ten miles an hour on over 600 miles of track. Finally, in misguided attempts to protect the public interest, the government had made it nearly impossible for railroads to prosper. Since the ICC had to approve rate increases, which usually aroused the ire of shippers, an inefficient railroad like the Milwaukee Road lost more money the more freight it moved.

When a company declares bankruptcy, all the cards are thrown down and a new hand can be drawn. Many institutions tend to dump their holdings (some of them are not even permitted to hold paper in bankrupt companies), which drives prices below a company's underlying value. Analysts tend to drop coverage as well, contributing to the confusion and hence the opportunity. The small commissions on bonds make them unattractive for many firms to trade, contributing to illiquidity and, again, further expanding opportunities for investors.

The Milwaukee Road was intriguing. It was a land-grant railroad, which meant that as an incentive to build to the West Coast, the railroad received from the government millions of acres of land adjoining the track in a checkerboard pattern. The railroad also provided access to some of the largest coal-producing areas of the West, making it a strategically important target for acquisition for healthy railroads. Should the ICC follow through on its intimation that it would remove impediments that prevented railroads from abandoning track and speed the approval of mergers, the Milwaukee Road might be a very valuable property indeed.

It also appealed to us because the railroad was relatively small, and we could assemble a sufficiently large position to have a say in the course of events. At first we bought the railroad's bonds, principally the first-mortgage bonds. The bonds stood first in line to collect if the railroad was liquidated. We started purchasing the bonds at prices ranging from 15 to 30 cents on the dollar, reasoning that it was highly likely that the assets were worth more than enough to pay off the bonds plus the interest that had been accruing since the company's bankruptcy.

Once we acquired a significant position, I traveled to Chicago to meet with the management of Chicago Milwaukee Company, the holding company that owned 96 percent of Milwaukee Road stock. I asked the company's accountants what they felt the railroad and its stock were worth. The answer came back promptly and unequivocally: zero. In fact, the holding company carried the railroad on its books at a token $1. The accountants' considered opinion was that liquidating the company would not yield enough money to pay off its debts, much less leave anything for the stockholders.

Management could not have been more wrong about the company's value. (So much for inside information.) In yet another testament to the role of perception in finance, the railroad's stock, deemed worthless by the holding company's accountants, would ultimately yield $150 per share. Without a doubt, the accountants and management were shortsighted, but I suspect something more was at work. The difference might be explained by the collision of worldviews, each of which was internally consistent.

Management executives looked to the past in their assessment of the railroad. They saw its wretched history of bankruptcy and losses, the thousands of miles of useless track, and the years of failed attempts at regulatory reform; from this they could only conclude that the Milwaukee Road was a failed railroad that could never be profitable. We looked at the same railroad and instead saw vast assets in real estate and machinery that could be sold. Where management saw endless regulation, rate restrictions, and union rules, we felt there was now the promise of change that would enable the railroad to prosper once again. Plus, there was the teasing glimpse of a new business implied by Schlesinger's speech on energy.

This same clash of worldviews occurs during periods of gentrification. In slums and ghettos, residents associate the neighborhood with crime and privation and can't wait to leave. The architect or builder buying the brownstone sees a valuable, once proud building that can be had for a song. This buyer has no memory of the area's unhappiness and instead focuses on its glorious future. The same principle applies to every transaction on the stock exchange: The buyer is looking to the future; the seller often is burdened by knowledge of the stock's history.

Of course, life is never simple. Neighborhoods can remain grim slums long past the dreams of would-be gentrifiers; I looked at property on the Bowery in the 1970s, and had I bought it, I would still be waiting for my windfall. Although the Milwaukee Road eventually proved to be an enormously profitable investment, it took far longer to come to fruition than my partners and I initially estimated. Moreover, it became profitable for reasons very different from the analysis that prompted our original investment, which had been spurred by our hunch that the railroad business would rebound.

For one thing, the energy crisis abated, and the government abandoned its plans to increase its use of coal. But just as events in the economy were conspiring to remove one impetus to our interest in railroads, our guess as to the government's intentions to improve their competitive situation paid off spectacularly.

In June 1980, the U.S. Congress passed the Staggers Act, which allowed railroads to take actions—abandon track, merge, and so forth—that previously had been so difficult. Instead of facing a future in which more business meant more losses, railroads now had the opportunity to streamline their operations and improve their ability to compete. They still operated under government regulations, to be sure—after all, railroads are part of the critical infrastructure of the nation—but it soon became clear that the Staggers Act presented the greatest opportunity for investors in railroads since the switch from steam to diesel a few decades earlier. I remembered a lesson learned from an old friend: It's better to be on the same side as the government.

The Staggers Act might be described as a "good caribou," an unanticipated event that works to the favor of investors. Even with this fortuitous event, however, it was by no means clear how to play this investment. For one thing, because the railroad was in bankruptcy, any plans for liquidation or sale had to be approved by the bankruptcy trustee, a federal judge, and the ICC, all of them charged with weighing the rights of investors against a variety of factors, including the welfare of employees and the communities the railroad served.

We had initially considered the Milwaukee Road as a relatively short-term investment that would pay off with the liquidation of the railroad's assets. But the bankruptcy trustee, an able man named Richard Ogilvie, a former governor of Illinois, refused to consider liquidation because he thought it was against the public interest. He did, however, permit the railroad to abandon or sell two-thirds of its nearly 10,000 miles of track. He also approved the sale of tens of thousands of acres of land the railroad had been granted when it first laid track. These actions stemmed the cash hemorrhage and made the railroad much more attractive as an acquisition.

We continually adapted our strategy to adjust for these changes. As it became apparent that the railroad would raise more than enough cash to pay the claims of the senior bonds, prices rose, and we liquidated our position. There was still room for the bonds to rise, but Todd Lang, our attorney, advised us that bankruptcy law tended to frown on investors who held major positions in both the stock and bonds of a company, and the stock was shaping up as a more promising play. For one thing, only about two million shares of stock in the holding company were outstanding at the time, and by bringing in partners, we could achieve a dominant equity position. The principle is that money tends to flow to equity once creditors are paid off, with back interest.

Oppenheimer put a good deal of money into acquiring the stock. At one point, we owned about 25 percent of the issue, purchased at an average cost of $25 a share. To gain more clout, we joined forces with savvy and knowledgeable investors like Peter Sharp. With Jerry Green, Sharp had bought the Carlyle Hotel, and they demonstrated great ingenuity in devising ways to unlock the hidden value in this landmark New York City property: They converted the hotel into a co-op, and by selling apartments, they paid off the purchase price and greatly increased the profitability of the property while putting up almost none of their own money.

I had told Sharp about Oppenheimer's interest in the Milwaukee Road during a plane trip to Florida, where we were partners in investing in a bankrupt land company (talk about long-term investments— now, twenty-five years later, I'm still chairman of the board of the company, Avatar, that emerged from this bankruptcy). Sharp was a tough negotiator. With Sharp and other partners, we eventually controlled more than 40 percent of the Milwaukee Road's common stock. Despite this position, we had only one seat on the board of directors and had to fight to prevent the board from diluting our interest.

Eventually our stock holdings gave us leverage to have a powerful voice in the disposition of the railroad. (Once it becomes clear that bankers and bondholders will be paid in full, they have no clout in a bankruptcy. This is called "cramming upward." Conversely, if debt holders can argue that their legal claims will not be fully met, they are often in a position to "cram down" shareholders, virtually wiping them out.) With creditors out of the game, the voice of equity would be that much more powerful, and as offers to buy the railroad started coming in, we frequently had to use that voice.

The campaign for the railroad involved a large cast of people who played crucial roles at various times. Besides Fingerhut, Cistero, and Sharp, there was my partner Jack Nash, who was periodically called on when the negotiations got tough.

No sooner had we achieved a dominant equity position than we had a close call. Ogilvie announced that he had signed a letter of intent to sell the Milwaukee Road to Grand Trunk Railroad (a division of the Canadian National Railroad) for nothing but its assumption of Milwaukee's $253 million in debt, and $100 million in loans and interest run up since 1979. We solicited other bidders in order to forestall Grand Trunk's bid.

We then fended off the Chicago and Northwestern Transportation Company (C&NW), whose management offered more than Grand Trunk but much less than we thought the assets were worth. We spent roughly $10 million on lawyers and experts evaluating the railroad and concluded that it was worth between $360 million and $670 million, far more than the initial bids of Grand Trunk and C&NW. But we weren't finished yet.

In 1984 the Soo Line (owned by Canadian Pacific) joined the fray, and the bidding escalated. Ogilvie valued Soo's final offer at $570.6 million, just a bit more than C&NW's bid as of April. Then in a spectacular move, C&NW raised its bid to $786 million, a sum that would have yielded more than $200 a share for a stock deemed worthless only a few years earlier. With our full support, Ogilvie recommended that bid to Thomas R. McMillen, the bankruptcy judge in the case, on October 17, 1984. On December 21, the ICC ruled 5–2 that the C&NW bid was in the public interest (although it reaffirmed its preference for the Soo Line), and we thought we were home free.

The Soo Line, however, still had some arrows in its quiver. Its lawyers argued before McMillen that C&NW's high bid price would necessitate the very dismemberment of the Milwaukee Road that the court had earlier rejected. Judge McMillen seemed very partial to Canadians. Before announcing his opinion, he noted how they had been a loyal ally in World War II and remarked that if there was a World War III, the United States would need all the friends it could get. I would bet that McMillen's was probably the only bankruptcy opinion written forty years after World War II that cited World War II national security issues as part of the logic of his decision. In any event, the Soo Line/Canadian Pacific group won the day. Despite McMillen's allusions to national security, in all probability he was following the lead of the ICC and his own (accurate) appraisal of the relative strength of the two bidders.

In all, we fought off seven bids for the railroad as well as some moves by management, such as issuance of more stock, that would have hurt the interests of the shareholders. Our investment ultimately proved to be immensely profitable. Even after receiving $150 per share from the Soo Line, the holding company still owned valuable land. I was applying a technique I had learned from Sy Scheuer—to accumulate a large enough position to prevail.

Other investors were watching this battle as well, and as it continued, a number of players also took positions in the Milwaukee Road. One large investor who duplicated our position was a wealthy banker, the scion of a family-run banking business that had originated in the old Ottoman Empire. Because he was benefiting from the millions of dollars we poured into legal fees and research, I asked him if he would be willing to contribute to our expenses. He refused and, thoroughly miffed, I angrily exclaimed, "Now I know how they do business in Baghdad!"

We were not the only firm interested in bankruptcies. In the mid-1980s, a number of start-up investment companies and funds were launched with the mandate to invest in bankruptcies, and major firms like Goldman Sachs inaugurated their own "distressed securities" units.

One lesson from the Milwaukee Road experience was the importance of understanding the time frame of an investment. It was several years before the bonds and stock moved at all significantly, which meant that for a while the investment was a drag on our investors' return on capital. Negative impact of this sort can create pressures to bail out prematurely from a promising investment because there are always other opportunities competing for attention. Also at play is the phenomenon of "investor fatigue," to which all investors, including Jack Nash and me, are susceptible. After years of meetings and slogging through details with little to show for it, many investors want to flee and be rid of the problem forever.

As the market began to recognize that the Milwaukee Road had some value, another intriguing problem emerged. When a stock has tripled, the question for investors is whether to lock in gains or stay with it because there is additional upside potential. Some take a conservative approach. When criticized for selling his investments too early, the celebrated financier André Meyer of Lazard Frères replied, "Nobody ever went broke doubling his money." He's right, but from my point of view, the proper perspective on an investment is not what you have made so far, but rather the risk and reward ratio at any given point. The price you paid for a stock is irrelevant.

At Oppenheimer, there were always those who wanted to lock in profits, but we tended to stay with investments sometimes long after they doubled; conversely, we sometimes held on to a position too long when the stock was falling. We constantly reevaluated our position, of course, but as long as we believed that the returns by holding the stock measurably outweighed the risks, we were inclined to hold it. That also reduced our taxes. We didn't sell a single share of the Milwaukee Road until long after Canadian Pacific bought the railroad.

Even good investments will hit a period when market forces drive the value of a stock far below or far above what the investor thinks it's worth, but at any point the investor must evaluate the potential gains and perils and the time frame involved. This principle brings us back to psychology, because the interplay of thoughts and feelings that causes someone to buy or sell at any particular moment may involve factors far afield from the health of the company or the state of the market.

8

Unlocking Value

TAX CODES REFLECT the values of a society. It is no accident that the French produce great wine. The French tax code used to favor the producers of the spectacular first-growth wines, who were taxed at a lower rate than those who made *vin ordinaire*. The tax code thus gave producers an incentive to improve their wines. I have thought about the myriad ways in which money flows toward tax incentives and away from high taxes and have concluded that taxes play a profound role in shaping history. Give officials control of the tax code and they can change society, either deliberately through the wise use of incentives or, more commonly, inadvertently through a misunderstanding of how people react to taxes.

Until the 1990s, New York City taxed unincorporated businesses, a levy that fell most heavily on freelance writers, artists, actors, and other self-employed creative people just as they were becoming successful. Using the logic of a politburo, the city council legislated a tax on incomes above $60,000. The unintended effect on New York was to drive these people away just when they could have made a real contribution to the economy and life of the city.

Many evaded the tax, some ignored it, and some moved away, enriching other communities at New York's expense. Despite the occasional op-ed piece in *The New York Times*, the tax stayed on the books, proving another point: Once enacted, taxes are among the most durable things on earth.

Government ingenuity knows no bounds when it comes to taxation. Gabriel Ardant, a French historian, wrote a two-volume study, *Histoire de l'Impôt* (1971), tracing the role of taxation in history. I revived my high school French and, armed with a dictionary, struggled through the two volumes. I tried to make my life easier by offering to subsidize an English translation, but I could not find an American publisher willing to take on the project.

I waded through Ardant's book in part because Eugene Linden (my collaborator on this book) and I had begun researching a book on taxes as a force in history. We put it aside when it became apparent that such a project was a life's work. I thought it should be someone else's life. Still, perhaps someday a great and far-sighted publisher will beg us to return to that project.

On the one hand, governments are usually efficient at getting what they perceive to be their fair share of citizens' money. Ardant discovered that the tax authorities in ancient Egypt would wait for the highest flood of the Nile to do their assessments, because at those times livestock was crowded onto high ground, making it more difficult for farmers to hide wealth from the Pharaoh. On the other hand, the tax laws offer a cornucopia of opportunities for profit. When the U.S. government decided that uranium was a strategic metal, Congress loaded on tax incentives to encourage entrepreneurs to strike out and find the stuff.

A flat tax (of, say, 17 percent for all taxpayers) would be simpler, but it would also eliminate the government's ability to offer incentives for socially desirable activities. The greatest U.S. tax incentive allows the middle class to deduct the interest paid on mortgages. The argument for this is that home ownership builds stronger communities and should therefore be encouraged. In more practical terms, a house is the largest asset most families possess; imagine the voters' reaction to a congressman who tells his constituents that he has eliminated their most visible gift from the government.

The business equivalents of the mortgage-interest deduction are tax rules that vary the time over which a company can depreciate investment in plants and equipment. Depreciation is government's way of acknowledging that the decline in value of such investments is a cost of doing business, and by reducing the time over which such equipment can be depreciated, government grants larger deductions and thus encourages business spending on new equipment. Eliminating depreciation would deprive government of a powerful lever to stimulate investment.

Then there is philanthropy. A very bright line separates the United States from other nations in the degree to which we delegate to wealthy individuals control of the arts, education, science, and other social values that elsewhere are controlled by government. We do this as a society through tax deductions for charitable donations and other tax breaks that encourage Americans not only to give generously during their lifetime but also to give from their estates after they die. What would happen to universities, museums, symphonies, dance theaters, environmental groups, hospitals, medical foundations, libraries—the list is endless—were the government to eliminate one of the prime incentives for making donations? Religious groups and property also benefit enormously from tax breaks. What politician would want these ordinarily peace-loving institutions to rise up against them?

People may yearn for the simplicity of a flat tax, but the chorus quickly grows faint when different constituencies size up what it would mean for them. Perhaps the major hurdle to passage of a flat tax is that it would require a citizenry already cynical about government motives to accept the premise that our elected leaders would keep the flat tax flat and hold it at 17 percent (or whatever figure was chosen).

In 1978, soon after I first realized that taxes were a social force in history, Eugene Linden and I arranged a meeting with Wilbur Mills, who had been one of the most powerful men in Congress and a leading expert on taxes, having chaired the House Ways and Means Committee for sixteen years. When I met with him, he had left Congress after the disgrace of being caught frolicking with a stripper named Fanne Foxe in Washington's Tidal Basin area. He may have had questionable taste in drinking companions, but there was absolutely nothing wrong with Mills's mind. I was very impressed with his understanding of the political and social context of taxes. He felt strongly that only someone completely naive about how Washington works could seriously propose a flat tax. Regardless of the pitch used to sell the tax to the public, Congress would treat the new lowered rate as merely a new base from which to jack up rates. After all, what taxpayers whose rate dropped from 30 percent to 17 percent would complain if Congress needed to ratchet it up a tiny bit to 18 percent in order to pay for health care for the orphaned infants of war veterans and police officers? And then the next year, who would complain about another quarter percent increase to bolster the country's defenses against some previously unheard of rogue nation whose sultan had unaccountably turned rabidly anti-American and bought strategic missiles from Russia or China? And so on.

In the 1970s, taxes on individuals and businesses were extraordinarily high, encouraging creative tax advisers to devise new plans to avoid them. Because taxes were so high and the stock market was so flat, incentive was lacking for businesspeople to sell their companies. So when my colleagues and I at Oppenheimer heard about a way to sell a company for a high price yet pay a low tax, we thought we had found an opportunity.

Ira Heckler, a brilliant Harvard graduate and CPA who understood the tax code, first brought the idea of the leveraged buyout (LBO) to our attention. Heckler was a creative entrepreneur in real estate, where an LBO is called "mortgaging out." The concept is simple: In an LBO, the buyer purchases a company by borrowing against its assets to finance the transaction. In practice, an LBO is much more complicated, because the deal must offer incentives for the owners to sell, incentives for management to excel, and a rich return for the buyer to justify time and effort. It sometimes took ten years to fully realize the value of the acquisition.

Even in its early crude stages, we recognized the potential of Heckler's idea. We struck a deal with him under which he would scout for underpriced companies with strong management and good cash flow in stable markets. Of the deals we did together, Heckler got one-third and Oppenheimer kept two-thirds.

I also noticed that with the market going nowhere, conglomerates were often valued far below the sum of their parts. This led me to believe that the merger mania of the 1960s and 1970s was ending, and we were entering a new period of disaggregation.

The LBO offered something for everybody. Shareholders got a price well above the trading range of the stock and, equally important, the promise that their gains would be sheltered from the tax authorities. The proceeds from the sale of the company would go into a mutual fund that invested in municipal bonds, which meant that owners could be patient and strategic in the way they drew down their gains: they postponed the capital gains tax and the interest on municipal bonds was tax-free.

We offered management executives 20 percent of future profits and gave them positions in a partnership with the right to manage the business for ten to fifteen years, neutralizing potential distrust and opposition. This concession was a major mistake. We thought that if we shared the same interest as management, the LBO would work out well for all of us. Were we ever wrong. In retrospect, the management contracts for the LBOs were a bad idea, if only because they meant we couldn't fire anyone. (A similar pitfall has surfaced more recently, as company directors have assumed, erroneously, that stock options created the same identity of interest with managers. Any reader of the financial news knows that this premise has proved incorrect.)

The first company we bought was Big Bear Stores, a midwestern supermarket chain that we acquired for $35 million in 1975. We put the company's inventory on a last-in, first-out accounting basis, which had the effect of raising our costs and thus entitling the company to a large refund of taxes paid in previous years. (The IRS still extracted its pound of flesh when the inventory later was sold at market price.)

The new streamlined Big Bear became quite profitable. Fourteen years after we first considered buying the company, we sold it to Penn Traffic. Since we had borrowed most of the money to buy Big Bear, our return on the investment was extraordinary, around 100 to 1. Because we put up so little money, the equity we invested in LBOs was like a warrant to make money. As every real estate agent knows, the tactic of borrowing money "nonrecourse" (without personal liability) with high leverage, when it works, has always been a way of getting rich. When it doesn't work, buyers lose only what they put up.

Long before we realized gains on Big Bear, we knew the LBO matched our mix of temperaments and talents very well. Ira Heckler loved making deals but couldn't care less about running the business once the deal was done. But the LBO was an investment that required just as much work after the deal was done (if not more, in some cases), because we had to run the company. Jack Nash stayed on top of the companies, ensuring that they were well managed. I participated in this work as well. I joined the board of Big Bear and became involved with the company's management. During this period, I saw as much of a small section of Columbus, Ohio (company headquarters), as I wanted to see. But not every LBO worked out as Big Bear did. Supermarkets are a highly competitive business, and we were unable to repeat our success when we acquired other supermarket chains.

I was patient and strategic about unlocking value. Waiting ten years to make 100 times our money seemed like a reasonable investment of time. Jack Nash had a much shorter time frame, but supported my ideas if I could put together a convincing case. We also had the expert knowledge of gifted tax lawyers like Martin Rabinowitz, who first advised us from his position at Weil, Gotshal & Manges, and then, after watching us profit handsomely on his advice, wisely joined us as a partner.

After Big Bear Stores, the deals came thick and fast. Some were consumer brands like Havatampa Cigar; others were more obscure. There were textile companies Shirley of Atlanta and J. P. Stevens; dress manufacturer Leslie Fay and women's apparel company Don Kenney; Reliable Stores, a chain of furniture and jewelry stores; and the discount chain Caldor's. Not all were winners, and many of the companies that we sold failed some years later.

As time passed, the government eliminated some of the incentives that made the LBO so attractive. One of the first plums to go was the device that enabled us to shelter gains from taxes through the creation of a mutual fund that invested in municipal bonds. By then, however, the LBO had taken on a life of its own.

Even as we explored ways of unlocking the value of underappreciated companies, I began to think about freeing myself and my partners from the day-to-day responsibilities of running a rapidly expanding company. By 1977, Oppenheimer had more than 1,000 employees, a thriving brokerage business, and the rapidly growing Oppenheimer Funds. These factors weighed heavily on our ability to move nimbly on private deals like LBOs.

There was always the risk that the deal side of the business might make enemies who would take out their anger on Oppenheimer's brokerage business. Also, management issues consumed a lot of our energy that might have gone into deals. To pursue LBOs, we needed permanent capital. Finally, the larger we grew, the more we became aware that the partnership structure of Oppenheimer exposed our general partners to unlimited liability if someone messed up badly.

We needed to segregate the dealmaking part of Oppenheimer from its other operations, both to free capital for private deals and to prevent any contagion from spilling in either direction. To this end, we needed a new partner willing to make a subordinated loan in return for a chunk of the private equity side of Oppenheimer. The idea was to set up a holding partnership that held stock in the management company, the Oppenheimer Funds, and other divisions.

After surveying the marketplace for such capital, I decided that the best place to look would be Europe, where a number of investment houses were seeking opportunities to increase their presence in the huge, dynamic U.S. markets. Eventually, we found a partner in the UK—Electra Trust, an investment firm run by Michael Stoddardt.

Finding the loan was only part of the battle; we also had to convince our co-owners to relinquish their partnership stakes in return for stock. Again, Jack Nash proved to be critical to the future of the company. He sold skeptical partners on the virtues of the new structure—an important task that I would never have been able to accomplish.

With this new corporate structure, we could more easily bring in limited partners and more aggressively look for deals. It was a well-timed move, because the market was changing rapidly. As the deals grew in size, Wall Street became interested in LBOs because of their rich potential for fees.

No one can see what lies beyond a fork in the road ahead before committing to a turn. Restructuring our company not only helped me to focus on making deals but also made me assess how I enjoyed spending my day. One side effect of the reorganization was that Oppenheimer now had a structure that enabled us to consider selling part or all of the business.

During the next few years, events conspired to make Jack and me (as well as the other senior partners) take this possibility more and more seriously. I felt great loyalty to a firm that I had helped build almost from its inception, but I had always favored traveling light. Both Jack and I preferred to be principals rather than agents, and the sale of Oppenheimer would free us to devote our energy to deals and market opportunities.

The market itself created opportunities for the sale of Oppenheimer. Foreign interest in the American market continued to increase, as various firms made investments in companies such as Drexel Burnham Lambert, First Boston, and Donaldson, Lufkin & Jenrette. A foreign buyer would likely pay a premium for a company like Oppenheimer with its blue-chip research department, high-performing mutual funds, and solid brokerage business. For Oppenheimer, a foreign partner could increase our penetration of overseas markets.

When we decided to sell the company in 1981, I first approached

Jacob Rothschild. In the back of my mind was the pleased look I imagined on the face of my late grandfather, who had emigrated from Poland. Rothschild was a name he would have recognized. Jacob demurred, but with the help of Michael Stoddardt, we eventually found what seemed to be a good match with London's Mercantile House, a worldwide financial services firm run by a prickly entrepreneur named John Barkshire.

Mercantile got everything in the sale except for Jack, me, and the other partners involved in corporate finance. We got the freedom to start fresh with a nice war chest. The sale held great potential for Mercantile, since it closed in 1982, just as the longest bull market in history began. The fact that Oppenheimer, by now renowned for its deals, should sell itself captured the attention of the press. An article in *The New York Times* was headlined "Big Oppenheimer Deal: Its Sale." The sale pleased everyone—except my mother-in-law, who called my wife the day the *Times* article appeared to ask what I was going to do now that I was out of a job.

The lucrative sale (for $162 million, which was 3.4 times the firm's book value) was marred by only one incident. We had hired Lazard Frères to sell Oppenheimer. As part of this process, the Lazard people undertook due diligence, and with the vantage point of an inside look at our operations, they began wooing some of the firm's best and brightest. To me, this was an outrageous breach of ethics. I also felt an obligation to Mercantile to deliver what it had paid for, and so I sought a meeting with Felix Rohatyn, one of Lazard's senior partners in New York, to get his colleagues to stop this incursion.

We met at Oppenheimer's offices on Madison Avenue and 47th Street. Among the people accompanying me was my partner Steve Robert, who was then president of Oppenheimer. He would be staying on with Mercantile, and as such was the principal victim of

Lazard's bad behavior. At one point in the conversation, Rohatyn tried to deflect our ire, saying, "Look, this conversation is going nowhere. All of us have been through a divorce, right? Well, this is like any divorce where you have different sides." At this point, Steve jumped in, saying, "You're right, it's like a divorce, but it's like a divorce in which your lawyer is sleeping with your wife."

The Oppenheimer-Mercantile match did not result in a divorce, but it was not a happy marriage. Oppenheimer made record profits that first year, but Mercantile was not good at managing the amalgamated company and felt intense competitive pressure from other financial giants. In 1990, Mercantile went bankrupt. Steve Robert and another former partner, Nate Gancher, bought Oppenheimer, ran it brilliantly, and after several years sold it to the Canadian Industrial Bank of Commerce. CIBC turned out to be highly bureaucratic, leading Steve to remark that "Canada seems to be a country populated entirely with vice presidents." Steve and Nate then auctioned off the Oppenheimer Funds to Mass Mutual. Steve now devotes much of his time to academia as chancellor of Brown University, and Nate is chairman of the board of Tufts University.

Jack and I went on to form a hedge fund called Odyssey Partners. But unlike many hedge funds that have a specialized investment style, we put no up-front restrictions on where we would invest. Why blind ourselves to opportunity, after all?

There are not many other partnerships that engage in both private equity and hedge fund trading under one roof. Ungainly as it may seem, the mixture proved to be enormously successful. We averaged 28 percent annual returns during Odyssey's fourteen-year life.

On the private equity side of Odyssey, we continued to explore the possibilities for profit in the disaggregation of conglomerates and other businesses. By personality, I was averse to hostile takeovers and nasty proxy fights. I've always felt that it is easiest to row a boat when everybody is pulling in the same direction. However, some of the conglomerates we analyzed as candidates for disaggregation were simply too big for outright purchase through an LBO (at least in 1982, before the advent of the junk bond).

We found an alternative to LBOs or proxy battles. Todd Lang, our lawyer and adviser since the 1960s, suggested that we try the "precatory proposal," a recommendation to the company that it take a particular action, but a recommendation the company would have to put before the shareholders. The company could ignore the suggestion, but that would be imprudent if it was supported by a majority of the shareholders. Still, the precatory proposal did not lessen the ire of management.

Our research department continued to study the companies that were selling at the largest discount from their business value. In this way we came upon Trans World Corporation, which owned the airline TWA, the hotel chain Hilton International, the real estate firm Century 21, and other independent businesses. The chairman, Ed Smart, was, from the point of view of TWC stockholders, badly named. The more we looked, the more appetizing TWC seemed. The stock was steeply undervalued, because the airlines had hit hard times during the deep recession of 1981–1982. In fact, TWC's market capitalization was about $500 million, less than the value of its Hilton International division. No single institution had a controlling position in TWC, but institutions collectively held 35 percent of the outstanding shares, which meant we did not have to seek out shareholders in the far corners of the globe. TWC had very little debt, and its five divisions were all operationally and financially independent, making their worth easier to evaluate and the company easier to split up.

Even before Odyssey was created, we began seeking partners to invest in TWC and put forward a "suggestion" to management that the parts were worth more than the whole. On August 13, the day I received a telegram telling me that Oppenheimer's sale to Mercantile House was final, I was having lunch with my wife and Sir Sigmund Warburg at a restaurant overlooking Lake Geneva in Vevey, Switzerland. He was very taken with the idea of disaggregation, and soon thereafter he joined an investment partnership we created to pursue the TWC breakup, bringing the French bank Paribas aboard as well.

While we prepared the precatory proposal (which was backed up by an exhaustive evaluation of the company prepared by the consulting firm Booz Allen & Hamilton), we tried to maintain secrecy. We were afraid our motives would be misunderstood and that management would create a hostile situation.

Naturally, this is exactly what happened—just as Jack Nash had warned me, although I had convinced him to go along with this deal. Word leaked out, and TWC retained Goldman Sachs to fight us off. They also hired Wachtell Lipton Rosen & Katz, a law firm legendary for its toughness.

Reacting to this new situation, we filed our SEC forms as required of shareholders who acquire more than 5 percent of a company's stock. We also declared publicly that we had no intention of taking over TWC. In addition, we disbanded the partnership we had set up to invest in TWC, freeing our investors to make their own decisions.

None of our mollifying gestures had the slightest effect on management, particularly Ed Smart. One of my big mistakes in this effort was underestimating the degree to which management believed it owned the company and did not have to operate in the shareholders' best interest. Anyone who followed the collapse of Enron would wonder how we could have been so naive. TWC's first public reaction to our approaches was to issue a press release telling Odyssey to "seek its opportunities elsewhere."

More to the point, management had at its disposal a weapon not available to smaller companies: a network of interdependencies and mutual interests with the board members and top executives of many other large firms. Whereas we were spending our own money, TWC could spend its shareholders' money with impunity. As a company that spent close to $5 billion a year (at that time), TWC was an important customer of many other businesses. Its directors sat on a total of forty boards. Through this network, TWC began pressuring the companies whose pension funds composed the assets of many of the institutions whose support we were seeking. TWC fought us on many other fronts as well—hauling us into court, and waging an ad campaign in *The Wall Street Journal* and *The New York Times*. The company also rammed through golden parachutes for management and changed the bylaws to make it more difficult for shareholders to influence corporate policy.

On the face of it, TWC's actions should have signaled to institutions holding its stock that management had something other than shareholder value as its top priority. But many of the institutions themselves had vested interests in keeping TWC together—directorships, perquisites (e.g., free airline travel), additional business from managing the subsidiary companies' pension funds—and the unions were strongly opposed to the breakup as well. Under pressure, some institutions that had promised to vote for the breakup changed sides, and others abstained. When it came to a vote, our suggestion got support from 6.8 million shares; management garnered 13.8 million. So much for my attempt at a friendly and civilized recommendation to management that would have benefited the shareholders.

In retrospect, I was the wrong guy to lead this effort. The precatory proposal was not a good idea. Without question, we should have aimed for complete control. I can blame only myself; I did not want bad publicity. When I was soliciting support from portfolio managers, they always asked, "If you lose, will you be back next year?" My answer was always a qualified yes, but it should have been "You better believe I will! And if we don't win then, we'll keep coming back until we do!"

There was one final irony in this saga. Throughout the drama, Goldman Sachs indefatigably argued that TWC had more value as a conglomerate than broken up. Yet Goldman seemed willing to argue both sides of this issue. Before signing on to defend TWC, Goldman had advised a number of institutions to invest in the company because of its breakup value. Moreover, in October 1982, at the very time we were assembling our partnership to unlock this value, Goldman issued a research report stating, "Separately, Trans World's non-airline assets are worth more than the corporation's total stock market value." Once Goldman helped defeat our bid, the stock slumped back into its doldrums, costing us—and Goldman clients who followed its research recommendations—a great deal of money. (This doublespeak was a precursor of the next decade when events revealed with brilliant clarity whom investment bankers really represent.) A few years later, with TWC in even more dire straits, Carl Icahn succeeded in mounting a successful takeover. He ruthlessly downsized the workforce and cut expenses so drastically (at one point eliminating regular aircraft cleanings) that he raised questions in consumer minds about the airline's safety.

Meanwhile, the LBO market continued to explode. As the 1980s progressed, transactions grew ever larger as firms put together consortiums to finance deals. Then, in the late 1970s, Michael Milken of Drexel Burnham Lambert started exploring the potential of junk bonds, an innovation that vastly expanded the universe of LBOs. Junk bonds were unsecured debt serviced by the cash flow of a company that paid very high interest to tempt buyers and that provided the cash through which to finance takeovers. With the advent of the junk bond, anybody who could create and move junk paper could do an LBO.

As junk bond holders are discovering today, however, the reward aspect of high interest rates is often offset by risk. The risk lies in the word "unsecured." If company cash flow is insufficient to service payments, the only things backing up junk paper are air, and the nebulous threat to senior secured bondholders that a junk default will hurt them as well.

Milken knew the risks of junk bonds as well as anybody, as became evident through the actions he took to ensure that issues were sold. He and his colleagues strongly encouraged issuers of new junk paper to buy other paper that his firm had created. Leaving nothing to chance, however, he also offered brokers who agreed to sell a junk issue various warrants convertible to stock at some point in the future. Since the warrants were completely extraneous to the issue and went only to those who moved the junk bonds, to me they appeared to be little more than a bribe.

Despite the abuses by Michael Milken and others, junk bonds are not inherently bad. Neither are LBOs, the use of options as incentives, or other financial innovations that have been used and abused in recent years. The flaw lies in how they are implemented and for what purpose.

9

The Pretty Efficient Market

LATE IN LIFE, I finally got around to reading the great nineteenth-century novel *War and Peace*. By all accounts, Tolstoy was meticulous in his research for this masterpiece. He visited battlefields and talked to soldiers who had participated in the Napoleonic campaign. From these conversations, he became convinced that the generals who planned the battles never really knew what was happening during the fog of war. Later, however, they would get together and reconstruct what had occurred, perhaps airbrushing or omitting the occasional embarrassing detail. This retrospective retelling would then become the official version of the campaign. All well and good—except for the minor point that the official version might be far afield of reality and thus a poor guide for generals preparing for future campaigns. So it is with markets.

Consider the collapse of Long-Term Capital Management (LTCM). Anyone with the most cursory interest in finance will recall the brief transit and violent collapse of this giant hedge fund in the fall of 1998. We had dissolved Odyssey Partners the year before, and I had the luxury of being a spectator rather than a participant. Like the generals observed by Tolstoy, the principals in this failed financial campaign somehow survived a great crisis without acknowledging a central lesson of their downfall: that the basic assumption of their strategy did not accord with reality. Moreover, in both cases, unanticipated human factors played a crucial role in obviating their carefully thought-through plans.

Like the ship *Titanic*, LTCM seemed unsinkable. Staffed by legendary traders and armed with an approach to the markets based on the specialized knowledge of Nobel Prize–winning economists, LTCM attracted a roster of backers that included the savviest veterans on Wall Street. After all, who better to find opportunities in the market for various options than Myron Scholes and Richard Merton, who just a year before LTCM's collapse shared the Nobel Prize in economics for their pioneering role in describing the pricing of derivatives—the very financial instruments in which the hedge fund invested? Uniting all the principals of the hedge fund were a supreme self-confidence and a belief in the efficiency and rationality of markets.

Initially, it seemed as though LTCM's rocket scientists had in fact uncovered the philosopher's stone. The fund made astonishing amounts of money. A dollar invested in 1994 was worth $2.40 just two years later. Major banks clamored to invest, but, acting prudently, John Meriwether and his partners had the discipline to resist the billions offered. They wanted the minimum amount of capital necessary to back up their trades, reasoning that the smaller the capital base, the larger the returns on capital.

Indeed, the partners did so many things right that the story takes on a tragic dimension. The principals limited outside capital, but many of them invested all their accumulated wealth in LTCM. This willingness to take personal risk stands in refreshing contrast to all too many Wall Street players. It wasn't greed or venality that brought down LTCM, but hubris, which blinded them to warning signals that their intricate strategy that churned and balanced hundreds of billions of dollars worth of financial instruments were based on faulty assumptions about the behavior of markets.

LTCM's strategy was to identify inefficiencies in the pricing of various options that companies, banks, and other large financial institutions use to reduce their exposure to risk in the markets. Over the years, Wall Street has introduced a variety of options—calls, puts, interest rate swaps—that give risk-averse investors the opportunity to sell off their potential gains or otherwise limit their potential losses in the currency, bond, and stock markets. A large company like IBM might limit or hedge its risk in the international currency markets by selling to someone else the opportunity to gain from wild movements of some of its positions in yen, euros, or pounds. The invisible hand of the market would price these derivatives (so-called because they are "derived" from another financial instrument) as various parties made their judgments of what they were willing to pay, given the risks and rewards each option entailed.

As these financial products proliferated, however, occasional price discrepancies emerged in options that were virtually identical. In such circumstances, a canny trader could sell the overpriced security or option, buy its underpriced twin, and make money as time and the workings of the marketplace eliminated this inefficiency. This strategy is called "arbitrage," and such transactions are viewed as virtually risk-free. Moreover, the arbitrage itself helps to eliminate the inefficiency (selling overpriced options helps drive the price down, while buying underpriced options creates upward pressure), and thus arbitrage is often defended as a policing mechanism that targets and removes unwarranted price discrepancies in the marketplace. (It is interesting to note that any profitable market strategy, no matter how obviously it is driven by greed, always is deemed good for society by those who reap the profits.)

The catch is that the price discrepancies targeted by arbitrageurs are often tiny: In one of LTCM's transactions, the premium on one bond that was slightly easier to sell than its equivalent was 0.3 percent, or roughly 1/300th of the value of the bond. To realize any meaningful gains on this transaction, an arbitrageur would have to buy a massive amount of bonds, and even then the transaction might be profitable only if the arbitrageur could borrow most of the money needed. For example, if you found a way to borrow 90 percent of the money needed, you could buy nine times the amount of bonds and realize roughly a 2.7 percent return on the money you invested; a 99 percent margin would yield a 27 percent return.

LTCM did even better than that. As masterminds of risk management, their strategists developed intricate ways to balance and otherwise offset risks to the point that they were able to borrow virtually all the money needed. When collateral was needed for a transaction, it would be transferred, but then moved again as soon as it could be freed up to support some other trade. At its height, the hedge fund had $4.72 billion of capital that served as collateral for $125 billion in bonds. And beyond this, LTCM controlled a portfolio of $1.25 trillion in derivatives. The enterprise was like one of those balancing acts perfected by the Chinese circus in which several acrobats maintain a precarious balance on the shoulders of one stout man nervously riding a bicycle.

LTCM was able to convince its bankers and partners to finance this astonishing leverage because the risk in each transaction was supposedly covered by collateral or mirrored in some way by other offsetting transactions. As long as the markets stayed within certain boundaries of volatility, LTCM's elaborate castle of 600,000 different positions produced outsized returns for the fund's investors. Moreover, had the LTCM crowd been content with smaller returns, the collapse of August 1998 might never have happened. But Meriwether, Scholes, and Merton were so confident about their formulas and risk assessments that they felt comfortable pushing this contraption to the limit, almost daring the market to prove them wrong. The aggressiveness of the fund ultimately tested the assumptions upon which LTCM had built its $1.25 trillion magical kingdom of transactions.

The fund's chutzpah was in its extraordinary leverage, which turned a risk-free strategy into a highly risky bet on the nature of the markets by serving as a giant magnifier. What ultimately did in LTCM was the difference between the reality of markets and the abstract model upon which the fund based its strategy. Magnified a thousand times, these subtle differences emerged as monsters. Creatures no more dangerous than a gecko for a company flush with capital instead ballooned into Tyrannosaurus Rex in the distorted, highly leveraged world of LTCM.

LTCM based its strategy on the efficient-market theory, which holds that at any given time, prices reflect all available information about a stock or bond. Should prices veer out of whack, normal forces will quickly restore equilibrium. This belief in efficient markets led LTCM's strategists to adopt certain assumptions: that they would easily be able to sell their securities (an aspect of markets called liquidity) and that different markets did not move together except when there was some real link between particular securities. Moreover, in the vast markets for currency futures, the strategists paid insufficient heed to the impact their actions had on the market.

This last oversight proved to be crucial. Not only did LTCM have an enormous portfolio, but other Wall Street firms were also involved in derivatives arbitrage, including a few firms that explicitly sought to emulate LTCM's trades. Often LTCM and like-minded hedge funds controlled large percentages of a particular bond issue or financial instrument.

But in a larger sense, LTCM failed to appreciate, or dismissed, the role of psychology in markets, a factor that hung over all its misunderstandings of the nature of the market. Finally, and perhaps most important, LTCM ignored a simple truism: You don't know what you don't know.

These misunderstandings and blind spots came to the surface in the late spring and summer of 1998 as financial markets began to unravel. Although Odyssey had been dissolved, I still helped oversee some nonprofit endowments (including the Institute for Advanced Study, the Guggenheim Foundation, Bard College, and the American Academy in Rome), and I was worried about the impact of market turmoil. To be prudent, I decided to sell off the portfolio of junk bonds in some of these endowments.

I reasoned that as fear took hold of the credit markets, the slaughter of value would be indiscriminate. Any financial paper that appeared to carry risk would be shunned as investors rushed to the redoubt of government bonds. Furthermore, once fear set in, an enormous number of large investors would be trying to crowd through a very small door. Thus I told our money managers to sell the bond holdings as quickly as possible and invest the proceeds in various U.S. government securities.

As for LTCM, with fear distorting prices in the derivatives market, the firm's generals suddenly found themselves in the fog of battle. And, as was the case with Napoleon's army nearly two centuries earlier, it was Russia that defeated the financial juggernaut. (It is ironic that Russia at its weakest proved more of a threat to the world financial architecture than the Soviet Union ever was at the height of its power and when it was bent on global domination.) In both cases, psychology proved critical. Napoleon's delusion was to believe in military strategy and underestimate the role of morale; his generals failed to appreciate that Russian citizens battling for their lives on their home soil had far greater incentive to fight than did a poilu from Paris yearning for the Champs Elysées. The LTCM strategists' delusion was to watch a market go mad and fail to appreciate the degree to which their own actions contributed to the insanity.

The crisis began in earnest on August 19, when Russia defaulted on payments on its bonds, and then placed a one-month moratorium on local bank payments on foreign currency contracts. In theory, LTCM should have been insulated against such events, since its Russian exposure was small, and in any event, its entire portfolio was balanced and hedged. Moreover, depleted and impoverished, Russia was an insignificant player on the world financial stage.

After the Russian decision, the cascade began when three European banks, feeling squeezed, took advantage of bankruptcy laws to halt payments to a large hedge fund appropriately named High-Risk Opportunities. As Nicholas Dunbar tells the story in his book on LTCM, *Inventing Money*, this forced the hedge fund into liquidation, which in turn increased the volatility of the markets. Most hedge funds involved in arbitrage used the same tools as LTCM to manage risks, which meant that as volatility increased beyond its expected range, many firms had to either find more capital or prune their portfolios. Since the easiest way to find additional capital was to liquidate the most marketable positions, the increased volatility set off a chain reaction of selling as funds started dumping the same derivatives into an already saturated market.

With dozens of hedge funds trying to flee the markets, the selling pressure sent prices haywire around the world. Erratic prices served only to increase volatility in the marketplace, forcing more funds to breach their tolerances of risk and sell, which further aggravated the madness.

Although LTCM's managers refused to acknowledge it, the market was rubbing their noses in their cherished assumptions. One assumption was that the price of a given security was independent of the prices of unrelated securities. With a diverse portfolio of investments, one bad apple shouldn't affect the others. But this diversity was an illusion. Apart from the copycat aspects of the market in the summer of 1998, even within LTCM there were linkages among different parts of its portfolio simply because trouble in the firm's capital position forced LTCM to liquidate its diverse positions to remain solvent. These positions may have been unrelated in other respects, but they had a common link to the financial stability of LTCM and other like-minded funds.

LTCM's Chinese acrobatic show was beginning to wobble as its frantic bicyclist maneuvered to keep the acrobats from falling on his head. In August alone, the fund lost roughly 45 percent of its capital, an event that the fund's risk analysis predicted should happen no more than once in the history of Western civilization. It shouldn't be unduly difficult to draw a conclusion about whether LTCM was extremely unlucky, or whether its managers misunderstood the nature of the risk.

Around this time, my wife Shelby and I were attending an anniversary dinner in New York for two European friends. Also present was Sanford Weill, then the CEO of Travelers. Weill was unusually distracted, and for good reason. The same bizarre moves in the credit markets that had convinced me to get the two endowments out of junk bonds were costing him money. Part of the vast Travelers portfolio of companies included Salomon Brothers, the investment banking firm, which at that time had a large arbitrage operation, in some respects similar to that of LTCM. After a reputed loss of $200 million the previous year, Weill had decided to close or sell this portfolio. But the firm botched the sale as rumors spread through the marketplace of what Travelers was up to, which cost another $100 million. Initially, LTCM had blamed its problems on investor reaction to Salomon's moves. On this Sunday evening, everybody was wondering whether the Fed would organize a bailout of LTCM, or whether the giant hedge fund might bring down the world financial system with it as it hurtled toward collapse.

The dinner had a déjà vu undercurrent. Eleven years earlier, on Friday, October 16, 1987, Shelby and I had dined with a group that included Robert Birnbaum, the president of the New York Stock Exchange, and Sidney Robbins, a professor of finance at Columbia University. That Friday was notable because the markets had swooned that day, and everybody was talking about what might happen on Monday. When the group asked me my opinion, I told them about one of my favorite plays, *Tiger at the Gates* by Jean Giraudoux. The play features characters discussing whether the Trojan War might be averted. Ulysses says that war cannot be averted, but Hector warns that the consequences of war are horrible, and a general should expend every effort to avert it. Just when it seems war has been avoided, news is carried to the stage of the death of a Greek soldier. The death must be avenged, and the closing lines in the play announce that "the Trojan War has begun." The play's message for me is that some events are inevitable. That Monday, October 19, the market crashed.

In September 1998, as in October 1987, liquidity, the lifeblood of markets, was disappearing from the exchanges. But psychology remained a crucial element. Since Argentina was not going bankrupt—at least not then—buyers should have been seizing the opportunity for quick profits as prices plunged. But as in 1987, buyers were nowhere to be found. To some degree, the reasons were practical— as LTCM teetered toward insolvency, no one knew how the forced liquidation of its enormous portfolio would affect prices, and traders in its markets pulled back. But everybody else pulled back as well, and some of the world's most liquid markets began to freeze up.

It's natural for people to pull back in times of uncertainty, but this largely emotional reaction has enormous effects on markets. In normal times, trades proceed smoothly in part because those on each side of the trade have confidence that the other party will honor its part of the bargain. But when markets go into a dive, one can't be sure whether the company on the other side of the deal is solvent. And once doubts enter the imagination, they spread rapidly and can quickly become paralyzing. The result is that anxiety about the health of the system makes those with capital extraordinarily fearful. Buyers become reluctant to enter the market, and lenders pull back as well.

Worried that the global financial system would completely freeze solid unless something was done to restore confidence in the markets, the U.S. Federal Reserve prodded a consortium of banks and investment houses to take over LTCM. This move allayed fears that the world's fragile markets would have to absorb a forced liquidation of LTCM's assets. Then the Fed lowered interest rates twice in a month—a signal that the United States stood ready to supply easy money to heal the wounds. LTCM's losses alone came to $4.6 billion, and the temporary damage to the world's markets reached trillions of dollars. The bailout may have prevented a complete collapse of the global financial order, but some markets still have not recovered from the scary events of the summer of 1998.

What can be made of this chain of events?

First and foremost, never have more than one Nobel laureate economist as a partner in a hedge fund. LTCM had two. Having had one Nobel prize winner as a limited partner over the years, I can say that had our firm followed his advice, we too might have lost a lot of money.

The LTCM episode also revealed that the market was not sufficiently efficient to justify the models devised by LTCM. That and the gyrations of hi-tech stocks in recent years reveal the efficient-market theory to be something of a misnomer. Instead of an efficient market, we have what we might call the pretty efficient market—a market that does integrate an enormous amount of information into realistic prices much of the time, but that is also prey to manic changes of mood at unpredictable moments. Imagine a repertory company that ordinarily performs Shakespeare, but one evening it treats the audience to a scene from *The Mikado*.

As LTCM began to tumble, the picture of the market began to change. As the debacle unfolded, the image of a rational, efficient system faded, and a moody, tempestuous market came into focus. LTCM was like a ship sailing smoothly, gradually finding itself in rougher and rougher waters and eventually engulfed by a typhoon. Rather than a system driven by natural economics, it had become a market driven by emotional and psychological factors. But if entire nations can be seized by manias—recall Germany in the 1930s—why should we assume that people will always behave rationally when they invest their money?

Although it was not clear at the time, the collapse of LTCM marked a more profound change of mood in the market as well. In the seven years leading up to August 1998, the spread between U.S. Treasury bonds and riskier bonds issued by corporations and emerging markets had been steadily narrowing. The credit market was saying, in effect, that times were so good that ordinary caution (as represented by higher rates for risky ventures or places) could be thrown to the wind. The narrowed spreads meant that cheap money was available to finance all sorts of new and growing enterprises in all sorts of places. Companies could issue so-called junk bonds to finance takeovers or expansions. And an irrationally exuberant stock market offered favored companies another easy way to raise money in order to grow by issuing more shares of their own stock.

This mood had been briefly darkened by the Asian financial crisis of 1997, when Thailand defaulted on its debt, setting off a chain reaction of panicked selling throughout Asia. Still, the credit markets had resumed their narrowing trend when the Russian default changed everything. As one trader put it, "That one month wiped out everything achieved in the past seven years."

Just before the Russian crisis, bonds in some emerging markets like China were priced at only 3 percent more than T-bills, an unusually small spread for, in China's case, an emerging, potentially unstable giant with a history of reneging on debts. In the aftermath of the Russian crisis, the spread widened first to 15 percent and then settled at 8 percent, a more realistic appraisal of China's prospects today given the many unknowns that cloud its future. Indeed, China is now looking a little better, so perhaps investors could find opportunities there.

Interestingly, spreads have not significantly narrowed since August 1998. Moreover, the junk bond market has all but ceased to function. As of this writing, the market is a fraction of the size it was before the Russian debacle. If I wanted to pursue a leveraged buyout of a company today, I would either have to put up more money myself, or give away more ownership of the company to greedy investment bankers. (At today's stock prices, though, I wouldn't want to do an LBO; there's a time for certain types of investments.) In the credit markets, lenders are more reluctant to lend, more judicious in those to whom they will lend, and less eager to accommodate those in trouble.

The change of mood among bankers has been matched by a similar mood shift among investors. Burned by rising defaults, many have pulled their money out of the junk market. Investment banks don't care much what they sell, but they do want their customers to come back tomorrow. For junk bonds, the buyers tend to be high-yield mutual funds, and if investors pull their money out of those funds, it matters little how energetic or persuasive the seller is.

In the credit market today, the image has shifted from a benign smile on the future to a tight frown of fear that has deeply affected both the stock market and the junk bond market. The years 2000–2002 were among the worst for equities since 1960. Still, most market observers (who failed to predict the downturn in the markets) failed to recognize the pitfalls facing consumers and investors and started looking for a market bottom under the assumption that the recession would be short and the markets would soon resume their inexorable rise to new heights. These analysts are going to be sorely disappointed.

The boom of the past decade was built on credit. Since the 1950s, the indebtedness of the U.S. economy has doubled. Now that bankers are more circumspect about lending, corporations founded in the past few years that are looking for the next round of financing will have a much harder time finding it, both in the market and from investors. The mood of the credit markets will have great bearing on thousands of fledgling companies. A boom that might survive higher interest rates — what does a 1 percent rise in rates mean if someone is expecting a 50 percent return? — might not survive the reduced availability of credit.

Thus, the collapse of LTCM may have a larger significance. Everybody thought that the Russian debacle and the demise of LTCM was a blip, a short-term problem in the markets that had been easily solved. This view gained popularity when the stock markets rebounded and hit new highs in the months following. But in reality, these events were emblematic of a sickness at the heart of the financial system, one that would infect the markets as the 1990s drew to a close.

10

False Profits

ANYONE WHO HAS BEEN around markets long enough recognizes a bubble when he sees one. In scale, the mania that gripped the American market in the late 1990s nearly matched the great bubbles of the past, such as the tulip bulb mania in Holland in the 1630s, the South Sea speculative frenzy of 1719 in England, the railway mania of 1845, and the Japanese real estate bubble of the 1980s. But the Internet bubble was all the more remarkable because it occurred in the most liquid, sophisticated, and ostensibly diverse market in history, and it continued to inflate despite a drumbeat of warnings in the mainstream press that laid out in the plainest possible language the absurdity of the valuations that investors were lavishing on stocks.

As the bubble deflated, investors began to snap out of their trance and ruefully look back on the myths, delusions, and outright lies they had cherished as truths when they were blinded by a rising market. As the dust cleared, an even more remarkable trend surfaced. As stock prices deflated, so did many of the numbers that had propped up their prices. By August 2001, losses by Nasdaq companies had essentially wiped out all profits for the five previous years, according to an analysis by *The Wall Street Journal*. Robert Barbera, the chief economist at Hoenig and Co., told the *Journal*, "With the benefit of hindsight, the late 1990s never happened."

Not only profits disappeared; profit margins vanished too. Profit margins are used to justify lofty price–earnings ratios. An analysis by my brother Jay and my nephew David at the Levy Forecasting Center showed that despite assertions that profit margins had increased by 20 percent in the 1990s, in reality they did not increase at all.

The great bubble of the 1990s was further inflated by a much publicized jump in productivity, a number that had lagged through the 1980s and early 1990s at about 1 percent. To the relief of technology cheerleaders, however, productivity gains began surging to about 2.5 percent annually by the late 1990s. The increase in productivity became one of the props of the so-called new economy, even converting such stalwarts as Alan Greenspan to the cause. (Greenspan contributed to the follies of the 1990s in other ways as well. Despite warning about "irrational exuberance," he did not raise margin requirements, and he championed the repeal of the Glass-Steagall Act.) Financial columnist Jim Grant blew the whistle on the myth of productivity growth, citing academic work showing that computers were the only industry in the 1990s that experienced growth, and even there the gains were possibly the product of creative accounting.

Part of the illusion of surging productivity came from the bull market itself. William Lewis of McKinsey and Company has pointed out that productivity statistics mistook a spending spree for increased efficiency. With seemingly insatiable consumers willing to buy higher-priced goods, those selling the goods looked more efficient because their revenues were rising without any increase in their workforce.

There was no end to the accountants' tricks. Price–earnings ratios (for those companies that had earnings) also turned out to be phony. Companies artificially pumped up earnings by treating ordinary expenses as extraordinary events (Enron, Cisco), by booking earnings and revenues long before they were realized (Computer Associates, Calpine), by including capital gains from investments in earnings (Microsoft, General Electric), by buying back stocks (IBM), and by omitting the effects of options granted to employees (Microsoft, AOL, Cisco, many others). The list goes on.

Even the intellectual underpinnings of the new economy proved to be illusory. One article of faith was that the Internet allowed companies to continuously monitor sales and supply chains so that inventories would never become lopsided and recessions would disappear. Then, in the first quarter of 2001, Cisco Systems, a bellwether company of the Internet (and for a brief time the most valuable company on earth with a market value of $590 billion), took a $2.25 billion pretax inventory charge. This was not supposed to happen, particularly to a company that supplied the very backbone of the Internet and telecom revolutions. If a company like Cisco could have inventory problems (probably because managers will do everything to achieve targets and earn bonuses regardless of market conditions), then maybe old-economy imbalances had not disappeared altogether.

By the summer of 2002, not only had trillions of dollars in wealth evaporated ($4 trillion in Nasdaq market values alone), but so too had most of the numbers that provided the underpinnings for the creation of that wealth in the first place. The wealth came and went so fast that many millionaires-for-a-day had no chance to spend their gains. To name but one of dozens of examples, Theglobe.com stock soared from its $9 IPO to $97 in a day, and then plunged to less than $1 in little more than a year. It was indeed as though the late 1990s never happened.

Except that the bubble did happen, and its legacy is like a wretched hangover. Long after the valuations of new-economy stocks collapsed, major companies continued to take significant writedowns of their assets—$40 billion for JDS Uniphase and $54 billion in the case of AOL Time Warner—to adjust their balance sheets for the vanished wealth of their investments. Moreover, without the prop of an irrational stock market, investors finally tuned in to the fantasy accounting that had become pervasive in American business, and they slaughtered stocks whose earnings came under suspicion.

The collective madness that seized investors in the 1990s provides the most persuasive evidence of the role of psychology in markets. After all, this was a period during which even the most sophisticated investors willingly suspended their sense of disbelief and, perhaps even more astonishing, dismissed facts and figures staring them in the face.

It helps to review the 1980s to put the bubble period in perspective. The crash of 1987 may have wiped out many people and a number of firms, but the markets quickly recovered from the 22 percent drop on October 19 and even finished the year with a gain. The Federal Reserve flooded the banks with liquidity and restored confidence in a system that was perilously close to meltdown the day after the crash, but the lingering effect of this timely intervention was to leave investors believing that the markets were less risky than was the case. The crash itself was written off as the result of an unforeseen and one-time catastrophe caused by computer selling in a risk-balancing strategy called portfolio insurance. As computer programs shorted stocks, driving down prices, fewer buyers showed up to buy the stocks being shorted, putting further downward pressure on prices. Many investors who bought immediately after the crash made a good deal of money in the next year or two, which helped make the saying "buy the dips" the stock market mantra of the 1990s.

Throughout the past decade, whenever markets hit a bad patch, some wise old hand would appear on television and patiently explain to nervous viewers that in the long run stocks have always outperformed other investments. Then the markets would soar to new highs, breeding armies of smug new converts to the buy-the-dips religion. One tenet of this new faith was that the Federal Reserve and Treasury Department had learned the lessons of the Depression and now had the tools to prevent panics from progressing to full-fledged depressions. Thus, even before the Internet came along, investors were encouraged to believe that stocks were not as risky as their long-term price movements would suggest.

Corporations and investment bankers were delighted with the public's newfound belief in the infallibility of Alan Greenspan and the automatic road to wealth promised by the stock markets. Suddenly, here was a huge population of investors willing to assume the risks inherent in stocks—through their purchases of mutual funds—and tie their fates to their employers' fortunes by accepting payments into retirement accounts in the form of company stock. Who could argue, since the appreciation of most stocks was outpacing conservative investments by a country mile? Companies took advantage of this gullibility to shovel stocks into the accounts of their workers every way they could.

Then came the Internet in the mid-1990s, and the notion of risk was seemingly consigned to the dustbin of history. The Internet famously promised a "new paradigm," giving anyone with moxie access to global markets, promising consumers the power to "name your own price" for everything from airline tickets to groceries, and offering businesses the allure of fantastic productivity improvements in everything from dealing with suppliers to lowering the costs of sales.

The old ways of valuing companies went out the window, as did the notion that stocks were inherently risky. A book called *Dow 36,000* argued that even as the Dow Jones Industrial Average pushed past 10,000, the market was vastly undervalued, since prices were discounted for more risk than was justified in an environment of low inflation and strong earnings growth. The authors (James Glassman and Kevin Hassett) maintained that equities carried no more risk than corporate bonds, and that as investors came to realize this, they would accept less return in dividend yields and bid up prices. To the authors, even the historically high price–earnings ratios of the late 1990s were ludicrously low.

For a while, the data seemed to back up these arguments. The productivity surge in the late 1990s seemed to validate the claim that years of investment in computers and other information technologies was finally paying off. Internet companies were deemed exempt from ordinary standards of accounting. Reporting profits was cause for shame, not pride, since profits indicated that the company's executives were not sufficiently focused on growth. The trick for an Internet company was to capture as many customers as possible, even if it was losing money on every sale.

There is an old joke about the wholesaler who steals market share by selling suits that cost him $100 for $90 each. His friend asks him, "So how do you make money?" "Simple," replies the wholesaler, "I make it up on volume!" This seemed to be Amazon.com's approach, which turned a joke into a badge of honor. Stranger still, Wall Street bought it. Amazon argued that once it achieved a preeminent position as the destination of choice for Internet shoppers, it could begin raising its prices and rake in the profits. So far the plan has not worked out that way.

It wasn't only the younger generation who believed the Internet would change the world. Walter Wriston, a distinguished former chairman of Citicorp, was a believer in the new economy. I was not—maybe because I've never used a computer. Wriston and I debated our differing views in the pages of *Forbes* magazine. (I later expanded many of my views in an interview with Jeff Madrick in *The New York Review of Books*.) Wriston argued that the Internet was fantastic for business because it enabled nimble retailers like Dell Computer to respond so quickly that they could get suppliers to finance their entire business. I replied that the Internet was merely a new kind of store, and that as with any new way of selling, others would enter the business, driving down margins. I used the analogy of supermarkets, which emerged in the 1930s, driving out corner grocery stores, only to have their profit margins attacked by discount stores, which in turn found it ever more difficult to remain profitable as others entered the business.

I told Wriston that this principle applied to Amazon.com as well, noting that it was difficult to imagine how many books they would have to sell to justify their market valuation (which peaked at about $42 billion). Wriston replied that books were only their first product, to which I rejoined, "When there are other products, there will be other Amazons."

Risks don't disappear from markets or businesses; they are merely transferred or sold. In the end, Amazon was nothing more than a mail-order house.

The mania extended far beyond the Internet. Putting money in Internet companies required investors to believe in a miraculous "new age," but even many non-Internet companies turned their backs on what were increasingly considered stuffy and outmoded notions about what constituted earnings. Traditional companies had plenty of tricks to help investors see green when there was only red.

As we now know, Enron and a host of other companies erased billions of dollars of debt from their books, with the acquiescence of many of Wall Street's best and brightest.

One device Enron used to mislead investors was a series of partnerships the company formed to protect itself against risks in its investment portfolio. The problem was that these so-called Raptor partnerships could cover those risks only if Enron's stock remained high, since the stock was the company's principal asset. But as the stock price slid throughout 2001, huge losses mounted in the Raptor partnerships, and Enron began a series of desperate and (it turned out) illegal maneuvers to prevent these losses from coming home to the company and causing further decline in the stock price. While this was going on, Wall Street's analyst community was oblivious, blinded by management's sunny forecasts. Indeed, according to one account in *The New York Times*, Enron management was so concerned about keeping up appearances for the benefit of Wall Street that during one visit by stock analysts, it packed its trading room with employees from other departments to create the illusion of a bustling operation.

Such brazen fraud is nothing new. In 1963 there was the "salad oil scandal," in which a man named Anthony De Angelis applied for multimillion-dollar loans based on his owning tanks of salad oil, which turned out to be filled with water. Among the victims of his deception were the Wall Street firm of Ira Haupt & Company, which went bankrupt as a result, and American Express, which lost more than $60 million and saw its stock price fall by half.

I have a theory that scoundrels are generally more charming than the rest of us. After all, they have to be able to purvey unattractive wares in the most attractive manner. A few years ago, my partner Jack Nash introduced me to one of the more engaging and articulate young men I had met in a long time. His name was Andrew Fastow, the chief financial officer of Enron. He outlined a partnership that, as I understood it, was created to help smooth the earnings of Enron by making investments outside the normal business of the company, and he strongly suggested there would be a high rate of return. I was charmed by Fastow. He was a delightful fellow, and I too invested in the partnership. Like so many others, I was fooled. The partnership was not what I thought it was. I thought it was legal. I also thought I was fairly good at sniffing out devious proposals; this time I wasn't.

The Enron collapse demonstrates that even large, highly scrutinized corporations can manipulate the perception of numbers right up to the brink of destruction. Reality intruded only because the banks that bankrolled Enron's shenanigans pulled the plug. Now, reality is likely to intrude on a host of other companies that enthusiastically took advantage of opportunities to artificially inflate earnings and move liabilities off their books. My friend Andrew Smithers, who writes for the *Evening Standard*, has a simple rule of thumb for estimating the size of this problem. He treats the rapid rise of debt in the financial sector, which has risen from 32 percent of private debt to 36 percent in just five years, as an indicator of how much corporate debt has been swept under the rug.

If time had stopped in March 2000, pundits would have had ample ammunition to argue that a new golden age had arrived. Companies still pushed a sunny picture of growth, earnings, productivity, and profits. The trajectory of the market certainly looked as if it was heading for Dow 36,000. The bull market was eighteen years old, and consumers were spending as if there were no tomorrow.

But the poison in the markets was working its way through the financial system like some epidemic that goes unnoticed until thousands fall ill. Investors shied from junk bond offerings, and banks started to take a harder look at the prospects of the companies they had been financing so freely. Though few people noticed it at the time, a key moment came in June 1999, when a Lehman Brothers bond analyst named Ravi Suria pointed out that the emperor of the Internet, Amazon.com, was nude.

Bond analysts are the worrywarts of the markets. They care only whether a company is generating enough cash to pay its debts. Suria studied Amazon's business, which lost more money the more it sold, and issued a report questioning whether the company could ever become profitable. Amazon officials dismissed the analysis, and Suria had to fight his own company to get it released, but the simple logic of his argument was an eye-opener for those investors who wanted to see it.

Then, in February 2001, Suria issued another research report. This time the issue was not profitability but Amazon's very viability as a going concern. Amazon.com, like many retailers, ended its fiscal year in January, when the company was flush with cash from the Christmas season. The bills would come due in January, but in the meantime, Amazon always appeared to end the year on an optimistic note. Until Ravi Suria blew the whistle, Amazon's way to deal with mounting losses was to issue either new stock or convertible bonds. In essence, it was capitalizing ordinary business expenses.

By this time, the mood of the market had changed, and investors were looking at Internet companies with jaundiced eyes. Putting aside arguments about site visits ("eyeballs") and revenue growth, they started researching whether companies were generating enough cash to service their debts. Despite this, the true believers in the new economy might have staved off their day of reckoning a bit longer but for one factor that drastically changed the equation for owning hi-tech stocks: a flood of stock entering the markets even as demand was drying up.

This situation was the reverse of the bubble frenzy, when many hi-tech stocks reached absurdly high prices largely because of artificial constraints on the supply of stock. When a company went public, its initial public offering might be only a small percentage of its authorized shares, with the bulk of shares reserved for private investors, management, and employee stock-option programs. Typically, insiders were allotted shares under lockup agreements that prohibited selling for periods ranging upward of six months. This temporary stock scarcity created the illusion of demand for a "hot" company.

To put this in context, consider the brief life of a fictional (but typical) Internet company. Say that a few dotcom fanatics and I decided in December 1999 to form an Internet company to sell our patented tulip bulbs that glow in the dark. We give the company the ironic and suitably edgy name of Dimbulb.com (to disguise the fact that the founder is over seventy years old) and offer 10 million shares to the public at $10 a share. We wisely choose Morgan Stanley as our banker, and prior to the offering, its star Internet analyst, Mary Meeker, provides a report stating that given the exploding incomes of yuppies and the hip nature of our product, the potential market for our phosphorescent plants is $1 billion. Furthermore, with our business plan to expand into glowing grass, hedges, and pets, we should be earning $6 a share by 2002. Suddenly, Morgan Stanley is besieged with orders. In March 2000, as the market reaches its peak, we go public, and the stock price skyrockets to $100 on the first day of trading.

The IPO nets Dimbulb.com $100 million, a nice piece of change for a company that has yet to sell its first biotech tulip. But that is mulch compared with the riches we are after. We have sold 10 million shares to the public, but we still hold 90 million shares in various lockups. Presto! The market value of the company is now $10 billion, equivalent to the typical market capitalization of a traditional retail company with $7.5 billion in sales and 7,500 employees. As long as we can keep the analysts and the public excited about the unlimited potential of glow-in-the-dark gardening, we can go back to the marketplace with secondary offerings whenever we need cash. So we start issuing a series of breathless press releases, many of them describing barter agreements with other Internet companies, which also have ridiculously high stock prices and are desperate to show some revenue.

Alas, problems begin for us a mere six months into our life as a public company. First, Microsoft announces that it is entering the glow-in-the-dark gardening field, noting that it will put an icon with a direct link to its catalogue on every new copy of its forthcoming product, Windows XP. Publicly, we state that we welcome Microsoft's validation of the market for our products. Privately, half our executives start making discreet calls to Redmond, Washington, asking about job opportunities. Then an entomologist releases a study suggesting that our tulip bulbs will lead to the extinction of fireflies as the bugs try to mate with plants rather than each other. We immediately question the science of the study, while with less fanfare the top tier of the company leadership starts selling shares under the guise of "portfolio diversification."

My director of marketing knows better than anyone the minuscule profit potential of glow-in-the-dark gardening, and she's gearing up to start unloading her million shares. So are the founding CFO and COO, and I'm considering it too, because I know another 30 million shares are poised to come into the market, not to mention 40 million shares in options that we have granted in lieu of salary.

Unfortunately for us at Dimbulb.com, the rush for the exits begins to gather steam just as we need to go back to the market for more funding. Moreover, with the stock now at $4 a share, a secondary public offering is out of the question. The funders who shoveled cash at us a year ago are unwilling to cough up more, even though they're threatened with losing their entire investment if we go under. Indeed, some of our backers are pushing us to declare bankruptcy now while we still have a few million left from the IPO that they might get their hands on. And so Dimbulb.com flickers out, leaving behind embittered employees and investors but perhaps making the world a better place for fireflies.

For all of the assurances investors hear about the irrelevance of risk, the only real value of a stock is the estate remaining after a company is liquidated and the secured debt and other more senior obligations have been paid off. This was a truth I was taught in the 1940s, and investors had to learn this lesson anew in recent years.

Companies can maintain the illusion that operating earnings are real earnings for only so long. In a corporate replay of *The Picture of Dorian Gray*, earnings as depicted by press releases remained eternally ebullient, while hidden from public view was the true portrait that had become disfigured by warts, goiters, and pox. A company would report a radiant picture in its press release based on accounting gymnastics that focused on cash flow, while ignoring or relegating to a footnote anything that might cast a shadow. In October 2001, Computer Associates, one of the world's largest software companies, reported "pro forma" income of $359 million for its fiscal second quarter, a healthy 57 percent increase over the previous year. The glowing numbers were the result of a new business model, which stretched software revenues over the life of a contract. At the same time, the company reported to the SEC a loss of $291 million for the quarter using generally accepted accounting principles. Which number more likely reflected the future prospects of the company? Investors have since sadly found out.

No matter how powerful the company, eventually these discrepancies must be resolved. As the case of Enron has underscored, the consequences are not pretty. In fact, Enron was still on target to meet its pro forma earnings predictions as late as November 2001, even as the company's stock price was collapsing and it had entered a free fall toward bankruptcy. As Floyd Norris of *The New York Times* noted, "It managed to go broke without ever reporting a bad quarter." If anything underscores the absurdity of accounting abuses during the 1990s, it is the surreal image of companies filing for bankruptcy shortly after they pay out bonuses to management for meeting targets for operating earnings.

The bonuses explain why executives perpetrate these frauds. They were able to get away with them, however, only because ordinary investors believed they were getting rich too.

A final irony of the bubble market appeared in a recent study by Risk Metrics of 89,000 stock reports issued at Wall Street's largest firms since September 1998. The study revealed that investors would have done better by ignoring stock analysts' recommendations and buying those stocks that were least favored. Stocks rated "hold" (Wall Street's polite code for "sell immediately!" or, perhaps more accurately, "we sold last week") outperformed those with "strong buy" recommendations. In other words, the best strategy was to do the opposite of what the highly paid stock gurus suggested.

Apart from the usual conflicts of interest, and the herd mentality that causes analysts to push overpriced stocks at their peak, there are also technical reasons for the dismal performance investors get when they follow an analyst's recommendation. Whenever an analyst recommends a stock, you can be sure that his firm's salespeople have already been using the recommendation to push the stock. Thus there is usually a long line of people who have bought the stock before you, pushing up its price. Conversely, when it comes time to sell, there will likely be a long line of people ahead of you, pushing down the price. The more influential the analyst, the more likely the

fall, simply because in the perverse world of markets, if enough people believe fervently in a company, they are usually wrong.

One powerful impetus toward overly optimistic forecasts lies in
the very size of the institutions that employ the analyst. If you are
the chief stock strategist for a huge firm like Goldman Sachs,
Morgan Stanley, or Credit Suisse First Boston, you put your job at
risk if you make a pessimistic public statement about the future of
the markets. These giant institutions depend on a public that
believes in ever-rising stock prices for everything from their lucrative
IPO business to their retail accounts. Little wonder, then, that the
strategists of these financial giants almost always predict that stock
prices will rise in the coming year, no matter what their private opinion might be.

At the beginning of 2001, when *The Wall Street Journal* polled the
chief strategists of nine of the largest Wall Street firms for their predictions of the course of the market in the coming year, the S&P 500
index stood at about 1350, down from its all-time high of 1527 during
the previous year. The most pessimistic of the forecasters, Steve Gal-
braith, predicted that the S&P would finish the year between 1225
and 1375 (covering his bets nicely). Other estimates ranged as high
as 1715.

If you had averaged these predictions in January 2001, you would
have seen that the collective wisdom of Wall Street had estimated
that in the coming year the S&P would rise from 1350 to 1515, a nice
12 percent return. Instead, the index dropped to 1148 on December
31, 2001, a 13 percent loss. But for 2002, after being wrong the previous two years, the strategists were still predicting on average a 12 percent gain for the year, putting the S&P at around 1290. But by late
July the S&P had fallen to 850, which meant that the market would
have to rally by more than 50 percent in five months to meet Wall
Street's best guess from January. It is also a safe prediction that wher-

ever the market ends up, the strategists will predict a rise for the year to come. Someday they will be right.

We calculate risks both statistically and emotionally. Before September 11, 2001, many Americans knew there was a high likelihood of a terrorist attack on our soil, but because no large-scale foreign-based attack had yet succeeded, that risk did not enter into decisions about daily life. Even insurers, whose very survival depends on an appropriate appraisal of risk, offered terrorism insurance at low premiums. (Warren Buffett has acknowledged that this oversight cost Berkshire Hathaway roughly $2.2 billion in losses in its insurance companies.)

In the aftermath of the attack, the perception of risk soared, even as the probable success rate of subsequent attacks dropped. Yes, terrorists may now have even more motivation to strike again, but America was most vulnerable before the attack when our guard was down. The detention of suspects and the hypervigilance of both the authorities and the public have served to lower the probability of terrorist success, no matter our emotional assessment of the situation.

An analogy to this reaction appears in investor behavior, particularly during the last stages of a great bull market, when perception of risk and actual risk are at opposite ends of the spectrum. At the peak of the 1990s bull market, some Harvard economic researchers asked a group of investors to forecast average annual returns for the next five years. The average answer was close to 18 percent, roughly three times the historical trend. Investors under the age of thirty were even more optimistic, predicting 25 percent annual growth for the next five years. Even the more sober group of investors over age fifty-five got caught up in the giddiness and predicted average returns of 11 percent for the next five years. Keep in mind that this was in the midst of an unprecedented bull market, when even a cursory acquaintance with historical trends would suggest that after so many years of extraordinary results, it would be extremely difficult to maintain the pace of rising prices.

As the markets slowly unwind, the question arises: Where would the markets be today if in fact the 1990s had never happened? In October 1990, the Nasdaq had bottomed out at 323. If the Nasdaq had grown thereafter in lockstep with the average increase in stock prices in the past century, it would have registered a 6 percent increase annually, and the index in August 2002 would be at about 650, rather than at 1315. Even if you accept the logic of the new-economy productivity gains and generously agree that these justify an average annual gain of 12 percent, that increase still leaves the Nasdaq index about 60 points shy of its level in August 2002.

My son-in-law, Lakshman Achuthan, is managing director of the Economic Cycle Research Institute in New York, a think tank that looks at long-term factors driving the economy. Lakshman's group analyzed the way in which stock prices tracked capitalized profits, which in simple terms are a company's latest earnings discounted by the latest interest rates. The analysts did this for the firms in the S&P 500, and their charts clearly show the beginnings of the bubble in 1997. As of the summer of 2002, the markets were still significantly overpriced. Lakshman performed the same analysis for other large economies and concluded that the best analogy for the U.S. stock market in the late 1990s was the Japanese market in the late 1980s — an ominous parallel, because after Japanese stock prices got back in line with capitalized earnings, so far they have not recovered to their previous highs.

All these strands of analysis point like a billboard in Times Square to the same message: Stock prices remain noticeably higher than they would be if the bubble of the late 1990s had never happened. In turn, this means that to some degree, the bubble continues.

How long can it continue? There were thirty bull markets in the past century, but only seven lasted more than 1,000 days. All three bull markets since 1984 have been longer than 1,000 days, however, and the only bear markets in that time (until the current one) have been among the shortest. The probability is that the market is due for a protracted bad stretch, interrupted by sharp but short rallies.

Where the present market decline ends may or may not be evident by the time this book is published, but if the markets are adjusting to the 6 percent annual appreciation in prices that held for most of the past century, it is entirely possible that they will continue to roll back until the gains of the late 1990s have been erased and then some. This would put the markets back at 1995 levels. Although such a retreat would be disastrous for investors who entered at the peak and for those who bought on margin, the overall decline would more closely parallel the 1970s than the Great Depression. Thus there is some good news in what statisticians call "reversion to the mean." Markets tend to overshoot in both directions. Just as we saw stock prices rise far beyond the value of the companies, we are likely to see the reverse. Stocks will then be undervalued, and there will be new opportunities for investors.

11

Investing Under the Influence

I AM ALWAYS CURIOUS about what people are thinking when they buy or sell a stock. My guess is that during the heyday of the bubble, as the Dow surged by over 20 percent a year and the Nasdaq skyrocketed, great numbers of buyers jumped on board worried about missing the train, thinking, "I'd better get in before the market goes up some more!" This psychology and its supporting legends—"the Internet has changed the world"; "buy the dips"—held right through the Asian meltdown, the Russian debacle, and the early years of the Internet bubble.

Consider an investor who bought Intel at $40 in June 1999 (these prices have been adjusted for subsequent splits). The stock dropped slightly, so he bought some more in the high $30s, and then some more again in early 2000 as it climbed toward its all-time high of $76 in June 2000. Then the price started to fall.

By then, he was reluctant to sell. In his mind, $76, the stock's high, had become its new base. As the months passed, the stock plunged through the $50s, $40s, and $30s. Still he didn't sell.

Instead, he blamed the decline on an "unwarranted reaction" (a common reason investors give for a decline in stock they own). His broker reinforced this, saying, "Who thought you'd ever get another chance to buy Intel at $30 a share?"

Assigning any real significance to these prices is pure nonsense, but many people do it. People even view the same price differently, depending on a stock's prior history. If you bought a stock at $1 and today it sells for $100, you would be happy about that—unless the price six months ago stood at $300. Then the $100 price today would be a calamity.

Those who study the psychology of markets would say that in your mind you had revalued the stock when it jumped to $300. Similarly, when you think that a $30 price for Intel stock has some intrinsic meaning because of your broker's suggestion, you are "anchoring," or giving the price a special significance that is not related to the stock's value.

If you are reluctant to sell, you are typical of American investors, who sell their winners and keep their losers. Investors do this because the act of selling at a loss is an admission that they were wrong. I tend to do the opposite. I dislike watching my losers week after week, and if I sell them, I get a tax loss to offset capital gains. (Then again, the market may be telling me I'm wrong.) Some people sell their winners because they have been told they should "rebalance" their portfolio. But the issue is not rebalancing; rather, it's balancing at every moment the risks and rewards of each investment. The market price of a stock in and of itself tells you nothing about its future

There are many reasons why selling your winners and keeping your losers is a bad investment strategy, but no rule applies all the time. At the last peak of the bull market in March 2000, this might have been the best course of action, since winners would likely have been tech stocks and the losers value stocks. You would have captured the gains of irrational exuberance and kept the downtrodden value stocks that fared somewhat better in subsequent months.

Richard Zeckhauser, a pioneer of behavioral economics at Harvard University, notes that our aversion to losses makes us dramatically distort probabilities. If a stock goes down, the odds that it will reverse itself are only one in four, but most people believe the stock will recover to the price at which they bought it. If my imaginary Internet biotech company Dimbulb.com had stayed in business long enough to have sales, it probably would not have met expectations the following year. The probability that it would have a good year following that bad year is only about 25 percent, but most investors who owned the stock typically would think the odds were much higher, closer to 50 percent or better.

Many other quirks distort investor perceptions. Simple inertia stops people from acting on blindingly clear signals that they should sell or buy. There may be huge downside risks in a stock portfolio, but people typically discount the risks on stocks they own. Reading a newspaper account of bad news at a company is much more likely to dissuade an investor from buying its stock than to cause someone who already owns the stock to dump it. This is called "status quo" bias, and psychologists have shown it at work in experiments in which a group of people are given an item and asked to name a price at which they will sell it. They typically name a much higher figure than when they are asked at what price they will buy the object.

Much has been made about the wisdom of "buy and hold"—but the truth is that sometimes this strategy is right and sometimes it's wrong. Whether to hold a stock is a judgment call about where the stock will sell at some time in the future. Nothing else matters. Even taxes, though a consideration, should not be the overriding one.

Consider again the hypothetical investor who first bought Intel at $40. What happens when Intel drops to $22 a share? Now, not only have our investor's gains evaporated, but he has lost more than half his investment. He remembers when the stock was at $76 and he didn't sell. It's been more than a year since the stock was at $40, and earnings are plunging everywhere. Rather than grasping the opportunity to buy more stock at a price last seen in 1998, he is wondering whether he might soon be seeing a rollback to 1995. So he now sells.

I have found myself in this position, worrying about a stock I own, and I have learned from bitter experience, when I decide to sell, not to sell a small part of my position but to sell at least a third or a half. So much psychic energy goes into changing your mind about something in which you once had great conviction that it's important to make a meaningful change. You will have saved your money, and if you find you were wrong, you can always buy back in.

After our Intel investor has relieved the anxiety of further losses by selling, his psychology shifts again. He is once more on the sidelines, watching and wondering whether he will miss the moment when the markets begin to recover. But which market?

Ordinarily, investors would be looking to jump back into stocks, but ordinary investors have suffered enormously in the past few years. In the 1930s, investors with fresh memories of the crash were very reluctant to return to stocks.

Despite recent declines, there is still a good deal of buoyancy and optimism in the markets, more so than is warranted by a world situation in which all major economies have weakened and are burdened by debt and other legacies of the spending spree of the 1990s. We are seeing a profound shift in mood as the investing public veers from a focus on rewards to a preoccupation with risk. Even if the numbers matched up perfectly with some earlier period, the way people perceive those numbers will be different, a change that will play havoc with market forecasts based on past patterns.

I suspect that this is a time when the game is changing. A bell certainly went off on September 11, but the changes were under way even before the terrorist attacks. Just as the late 1970s were a period when forces pushed for breaking up conglomerates to "liberate" value, I believe we are in for a protracted period when bonds will be favored over stocks. If we look at markets only for points of change (under the notion that if things remain stable, everything will be discounted), then this shift in the game presents an opportunity.

Although we might understand that individual investors get caught up in the froth, what about the pros? The pros, it turns out, are subject to all the flaws of the individual investor. In the 1990s, the same financial tsunami that was drowning the individual investor also caught the mutual fund manager. The pros were taken in by the numbers that flowed from corporate press releases—numbers that were often inflated, and in some cases were downright lies.

This tendency to believe what one is told is nothing new—and I'm talking about some very smart fellows. I invested with one hedge fund manager against whom everyone else looked like a genius. I had known him for years and had great confidence in his judgment—yet he lost 97 percent of the money he was managing. As I look back, it's hard to imagine how he kept justifying his decisions. In April 2002, he was still thumping the table for a company called Allegiance Telecom, which was selling for $2.65, down from its high, only a year before, of $110. The money manager remained enthusiastic about its prospects. "Their business model is ready to dance," he wrote to his investors. Apparently, it was the dance of death. Four months later, the stock had lost another 65 percent and was selling for 92 cents. Like many investors, this manager still couldn't let go; he felt that something rightfully his had been purloined.

Unlike the individual investor, the fund manager has someone looking over his shoulder, and he is being judged in comparison with every other manager in his category and against the performance of the market as a whole. He also has a very short time horizon, since he will be judged by quarterly (if not monthly or daily) results. On the one hand, if he sells at the peak and the market then tanks, he is a hero for a day. On the other hand, if he sells and the market continues to rise, he will be fired. From a psychological standpoint, the easiest strategy is to stick with what he has in his portfolio. In his mind, the most likely scenario is that he is right and that the stocks he has selected will rise. But in 2000–2002 the market continued to fall.

Earnings advisories and announcements make this problem worse. Analysts supposedly pore over these figures; they interview executives, customers, and competitors; they visit plants; they scour the academic and trade press for clues to trends in the sector. They then develop their estimate (until very recently, usually followed by a "strong buy" recommendation). Why is it, then, that earnings always seem to beat expectations by a penny or two a share?

The answer is that analysts permit earnings "guidance," which is controlled by the corporations, to influence their decisions, and they don't take the long view. Here is what so often happens (I owe the example to Harvard's Richard Zeckhauser): The analyst may study a bunch of numbers, but the most important factor shaping his thinking comes when he calls up the CEO of a company and says, "We're thinking 27 cents per share earnings for the next quarter." The CEO says, "I think that's a little high" and waxes authoritatively about why (the reasons give a rationale, but in any business, the rationale will be incomplete), and the analyst settles on 25 cents. Everybody goes home happy—the analyst has a number and a good story, and the CEO has a number he knows he can beat.

As I watched the madness in the 1990s, I kept remembering my father's work. Without profits, companies cannot continue to invest in new factories, they cannot continue to employ people, and sooner or later, no matter what anyone says, like London Bridge, they would all fall down. The bubble grew as people thought the economy could continue to boom without profits. It could not.

The collapse of energy giant Enron brought this issue before the investing public dramatically in the summer and fall of 2001. On July 23, just three months after the CEO, Jeffrey Skilling, had told analysts about the blue skies ahead for the corporation, Enron fell below one of the thresholds that allowed its partnerships to absorb expenses that ordinarily should have been carried on the company's books.

The company was doomed. Two weeks later, Skilling, who had been CEO for only six months and had been deeply involved in the Raptor partnerships, resigned. Even after Enron collapsed, when Skilling testified before Congress, he insisted that his resignation had nothing to do with the economic catastrophe looming before the company.

Skilling denied any knowledge of the imminent collapse of the company he headed, perhaps because he knew the role some of those same congressmen played in pushing through legislation that helped enable Enron and its accounting firm Arthur Andersen to mislead—and defraud—the public. One key piece of legislation was part of Newt Gingrich's "Contract with America" in 1995. Sold to the public as a way of limiting frivolous lawsuits, in fact it limited the liability of accounting firms and executives, thus paving the way for the egregiously optimistic forecasts by CEOs such as Jeffrey Skilling. Thus, when one of Skilling's inquisitors, Rep. Billy Tauzin, wondered how this outrage could have happened, he needed only to think of the $289,000 he received in contributions from the accounting industry (the largest of any congressman) and to remember those heady days of the so-called Republican Revolution when he championed the augustly named Private Securities Litigation Reform Act.

If there is a lesson in this saga, it is that good times produce bad numbers. Good times breed confidence, confidence breeds arrogance, and arrogance makes forecasts overly optimistic as executives begin to inhale their own perfume. Bad times then breed a caution that forces better disclosure, until good times return and, along with them, accounting laxity. This happened following the crash of 1929 when the U.S. government broke up the trusts that hid the losses of giant utility holding companies; it happened when many of the "Nifty Fifty" companies imploded in the early 1970s; it happened in the savings and loan crisis in the late 1980s; and it is happening now.

12

Betting on Economies Rather Than Stocks

WHEN IT COMES TO INVESTING, intuition and analysis are inextricably bound together. Intuition helped me see that during the mid–1970s the stock market had greatly underpriced the assets of many companies and that these values could be unlocked. After using intuition, however, I had to tackle the hard work of assessing the difference between the underlying value of corporate assets and the persistent undervaluation by the markets. The valuation of an asset changes over time. For example, the value of a luxury apartment building on Fifth Avenue lies less in what it cost to build it than in what buyers are willing to pay for apartments at any given time.

You can never tell from where an idea will spring, whether from an ancient historian, an art critic, an economist, a journalist, or even a politician. Recently my wife and I were vacationing on Lake Como in northern Italy, where we stayed in a hotel overlooking the water. We strolled from our hotel down to the town square every afternoon to a different restaurant and took boats to visit other towns. I loved it.

When it was time to leave, I began thinking how wonderful it would be to visit more often. Then I remembered that Peter Sharp had financed his purchase of the Carlyle Hotel and had put up very little of his own money. I thought, I could do that, too. That was the "Ah-ha!" experience. Now I have to figure out the how. My first step has been to consult an Italian lawyer. And because I like working with partners, I've been talking to a hotel management company.

Over the years, I've had enough bad experiences and made enough mistakes that most of my enthusiasms evaporate quickly when exposed to bright sunlight. Still, having a reason to return to Lake Como is sufficient impetus for me to start the long process that could lead to a deal.

Lately I've been mulling over the prospect of investing in India, China, and Russia. I don't know if it was reading Tolstoy or finding myself with an Indian-American son-in-law that led me in this direction, but there I am. I expect the current U.S. bear market to be protracted and deep, but eventually we will come out of it. When we do, however, the next bull market will be different from what came before. Perhaps the next great run-up will be in these economies, which together account for more than one-third of the world's population and each of which did not participate in the last boom. Each has enormous potential, but each has huge unknowns that would scare off most reasonable investors.

Consider Russia: Will the government guarantee property rights and establish the rule of law? A look at Russia's past is not reassuring, since its governments, like China's, have a history of reneging on sovereign debt. In recent years, even when Western investors have had some success, all too often their profitable ventures have been expropriated by fiat or force. Will Russia continue to reform its tax system so that companies can do business without being vulnerable to the predation of corrupt tax authorities? They've already adopted a flat tax, contrary to the advice I would have given.

Even if the answer to these questions is a resounding yes, an equally important question remains: When? Before the September 11 attacks, the answer might have been longer in forthcoming than it is now, since the hunt for Osama bin Laden offered Russia a historic opportunity to overcome distrust and forge closer economic ties to the United States and Europe.

If Russia sticks to a schedule of meaningful reform in the next five years, money will flow back into its markets. They are now so illiquid and small that even meager flows might yield disproportionate returns. As of this writing, stock on the Russian market is selling at about two times earnings (excluding the major oil companies), a price that reflects the unfamiliarity of international investors with Russia. If Russian reforms can reduce this discount from other markets, however, it is not unreasonable to expect that stocks might one day sell for five times earnings (still a fraction of the lofty price–earnings ratio in the U.S. stock markets). It's also not unreasonable to assume that with reform will come an inflow of investors and perhaps economic growth so that earnings will improve, compounding the impact of a rising price–earnings ratio. The large Russian companies' stocks have already started to climb.

Which market offers the better prospects—a U.S. market still priced for giddy earnings growth despite the likelihood of continuing descent into recession, or a Russian market priced for the end of the world, even as many of its fundamentals improve? Time will tell about this intuition.

My hunch on interest rates has indeed proved itself. Interest rates are a good indicator of the consensus on future prospects for the economy: If the economy is contracting, central bankers tend to lower interest rates to encourage investment and ease the pain of debt burdens. If an economy is rising, the bankers' fears shift from recession to the threat of inflation, and they tend to raise interest rates to prevent economic activity from becoming overheated. The consensus is evident in the interest rates the market assigns to futures contracts on various exchanges.

My favorite futures contract—the eurodollar call—illustrates my thinking when I make a decision to buy or sell. Although the eurodollar call is an extremely arcane investment vehicle, my argument was simplicity itself. I came to it without using a computer or a calculator, just applying a bit of economics learned from Dad and my brother Jay.

I first tested the eurodollar call market in 1994. Since the 1960s, I had periodically made investments based on the direction of interest rates when the market consensus differed from my appraisal of the future prospects of the economy. The eurodollar market offered an attractive way to make these investments.

A eurodollar is simply a dollar that has been transported overseas, whether by U.S. firms paying for imported goods, by foreigners buying dollars as a stable currency for their savings, or by governments accumulating dollars to bolster the value of their monetary reserves. If you are on an airplane flying from New York to London and you have a dollar in your pocket, you can magically transform that dollar into a eurodollar by depositing it in a commercial bank when you land at Heathrow.

The eurodollar market emerged in the 1970s when the United States was gripped by inflation and large sums of U.S. dollars moved offshore. The eurodollar market absorbed these stateless dollars so they could be traded easily without coming back to the United States and wreaking havoc with the world's monetary standard. A eurodollar call is a contract (called an option) that gives an investor the right to buy eurodollars at a specified time in the future.

When you buy an option, the most you can lose is the price paid at the outset, which is a tiny fraction of the principal amount. For example, my cost for a $1 million ninety-day futures contract at a 6 percent interest rate would be only about $750. The price of the option is determined by the market, and it rises or falls with variations in interest rates. If interest rates move up and stay up—above 6 percent in this example—my option will expire worthless and I'm out the $750. But if interest rates move down, the price of the eurodollar future will rise, and I will benefit from enormous leverage. Should interest rates drop from 6 percent to 5 percent, my call would likely rise to the neighborhood of $2,500, more than three times what I paid for it. (My niece Julie at first was upset when she made money in this market, because she thought her gains had come at the expense of some widow or orphan. I explained that the steely-eyed bankers who played this market were quite capable of taking care of themselves.)

For a large investor, the leverage on calls can be even greater. When traders know an investor is good for the money, they are willing to grant much greater margin, in which case my potential return could increase to as much as 16 to 1 if the market should turn in my direction. Even with the possibility of losing my initial investment, I judge the probability of a positive return at about 4 to 1, an excellent risk-to-reward ratio.

This potential is what makes the calls a cheap form of disaster insurance against an economic recession, which would lower the value of my other investments. A recession typically is accompanied by less construction, less demand for capital, and fewer borrowers competing for loans, and these factors lead governments to reduce interest rates to stimulate economies. There are exceptions, of course, and also many uncertainties, but it's a reasonable assumption that interest rates will decline. Eurodollar call contracts provide added leverage because when interest rates are falling, short-term rates tend to fall more than long-term rates.

These contracts have other beneficial features. Their leverage makes them highly volatile, and the value of the contract may rise or fall by as much as 12 percent in a single day. If the market starts moving in the direction of lower rates, prices may rise to attractive levels long before the expiration of my option, and I can sell off my position at a substantial profit. Further, the enormous size of the market insulates it somewhat from manipulation. On a typical day, more than 1 million 90-day contracts might trade, each with a nominal value of $1 million. Another plus is that the market is settled in cash. And because the settlement price is determined by an averaging of interest rates offered by thirteen major London banks, investors can have confidence that prices reflect the consensus of the market at any given point.

In essence, the eurodollar call is one of the most liquid plays on future interest rates, providing great leverage and limited exposure. I have moved away from stocks recently because I felt that the probabilities of making money from interest rate moves were higher than from overvalued stocks.

Understanding the facts that influence interest rates requires knowledge, experience, and an ability to weigh varying circumstances, but much of that information is available in the public domain or from institutions that track trades and the health of economies.

I learned to pay attention to connections between economic theory and daily events by watching my father investing according to his theories on the interplay of capital spending, profits, and the course of the economy. I never finished reading his book, but my brother did, and long after Dad died, I continued to turn to Jay, and then David as well, who have turned Dad's ideas into a set of tools for making economic predictions.

Using Dad's work as well as numerous other indicators, I became convinced in 2000 that a deep and protracted recession was coming. (My brother's work actually suggested that trouble was brewing even before that.) This was not the consensus of the market; in 2000 and 2001, the futures market was forecasting a sharp recovery. By the summer of 2000, I was expecting not only recession but also adverse impact on the still-inflated stock markets from stalled or slowed spending as rising debt levels and credit tightening caught up with businesses and consumers alike.

The market was thus predicting a sharp decline and sharp recovery in the U.S. economy—the so-called V-shaped curve. For reasons unrelated to the possibility of some future terrorist attack, I differed. In February 2001, I was expecting interest rates to fall as low as 3 percent by year-end (as it turned out, I was far too conservative). A drop to 3 percent would have made the $750 eurodollar contract worth about $3,575 when the dust settled.

I told several colleagues about my eurodollar plan, but few cared to follow—some because they may not have understood what I was up to, others because they reacted the way Max Oppenheimer did forty years earlier. (When I tried to encourage Max to broaden his investment horizons, he made it clear that the problem was not whether the idea was conservative or speculative but rather how it would appear to most investors.)

Already, there are signs that the smart money was taking a new look at Russia. In the fall of 2001, I attended a lunch at the Rockefeller Center Club convened by Jack Brimberg (brother of the late Robert Brimberg, better known to readers of *The Money Game* as Scarsdale Fats) to discuss Russia's prospects. More than a dozen representatives of hedge funds and private investment firms attended. Two years earlier, with the 1998 Russian default fresh in people's minds, I doubt that more than a couple of Wall Street players would have attended such a session. Time is everything in markets.

When the pressure is on, sometimes mere minutes can be an eternity. The Federal Reserve used to prepare books with precise instructions and phone numbers for Fed officials in the event of market meltdowns. Depending on the circumstances, the official would open the designated book to find instructions such as "Call Mr. Tohura at the Bank of Japan at such-and-such number and tell him the following ...." The notion was that during a market melt-down, time is so precious that an official can't be fumbling for a name or number or even pondering what to say.

I have witnessed a number of market meltdowns, either as victim, innocent bystander, or participant. During the culmination of George Soros's famous attack on the British pound on September 16, 1992, George was vilified in the British press as the "man who broke the Bank of England," but I felt then and still feel that he should have been granted a knighthood or been made a peer of the realm for his service to the British economy. The crucial time frame for this momentous event was one day.

This financial epic played out against the backdrop of the politi-cal maneuverings prior to creation of the euro. The UK at that time was positioning itself to enter the European Union. This meant that it had to keep its currency in line with the exchange rates estab-lished under the Maastricht Treaty. Typically, a government will strengthen its currency by raising interest rates, which attracts inflows of capital seeking the higher returns.

In 1992, however, the idea that Britain should raise interest rates was outright lunacy. The economy was hurting, and with the British pound at high levels relative to other markets, the country's export-ing industries were at a price disadvantage. British businesses thus suffered a double hurt of high interest rates (which dampen capital spending) and diminished export opportunities. Nonetheless, when Germany's Bundesbank raised its rates in response to the expenses of reinflating the economy of recently absorbed East Germany, the Bank of England followed suit.

The British government looked at its problem through a rear-view mirror. George Soros was looking ahead with vision and courage. He saw that the pound was overvalued and that the British treasury could not afford to support it indefinitely.

Once the pound fell, exporters would benefit, since their goods would be cheaper relative to other currencies and the Bank of England would have less incentive to artificially raise interest rates, aiding borrowers as well. George merely helped things along. Making a small investment, I went along for the ride.

Soros mounted an attack on the pound. A consortium of European banks had bought about $10 billion in pounds on behalf of the Bank of England. Soros approached the consortium and said he wanted to sell those $10 billion in pounds short—in essence borrowing pounds at the high current exchange rate. If the pound's value fell, he could repay with cheaper pounds and pocket the difference. The bankers saw what Soros was doing and realized that they could reap the rewards of benefiting from spreads on both sides of this transaction, so they allowed Soros to complete his massive short sale. Others were also shorting the pound, putting intolerable pressure on the Bank of England, which had to draw down its reserves of hard currency to purchase pounds to prevent devaluation.

The pound was doomed to fall. The UK's reserves of hard currency such as dollars (ultimately, the only backing for the pound) were plummeting. In the end, Britain capitulated and rescinded the interest rate hike, and allowed the pound to fall. In time, the normal workings of the economy brought about a recovery. The British government could have saved itself a lot of money if it had simply written Soros a check (he made $1 billion on September 16 alone). Better yet, it might have recognized the foolishness of trying to fight market forces and instead let the pound seek its own level. That kind of thinking is probably what lost them the thirteen colonies.

Governments are loath to do this, however, which creates great opportunities for investors. During the Asian financial crisis of 1997, the Thai government could have preempted any attack on its currency, the baht, by allowing it to fall when it became clear the Thai economy was weakening. (Thailand was at a competitive disadvantage to China and other Asian neighbors on labor costs, and during its boom years, it had drastically overbuilt.) Why didn't Thailand let the market work? The answer is obvious when we identify whom would be hurt by a devaluation. The segment of society most dependent on imports was the elite, and a devaluation would have raised their costs. Moreover, many of Thailand's most important businesses and families had debts denominated in dollars.

Instead of devaluing, the Bank of Thailand vowed to protect the value of the baht. This proved to be a fatal mistake, because the instrument it created to protect the baht gave speculators the very tool they needed to mount an attack on the currency. In early 1997, Thailand began selling futures contracts that promised to deliver dollars at a designated rate at different points in the future. Suddenly speculators had contracts that gave them the ability to short the currency in massive amounts.

By selling these contracts short (that is, they would have to pay the amount of baht at some future date), the speculators were betting that the Thai government would have to devalue the currency because it would not have the hard currency to satisfy the obligations the contracts entailed. Then the speculators could repay the contracts with cheaper currency and reap the difference as a profit.

It was obvious that Thailand could not possibly deliver on the promises entailed in the billions in futures contracts created by its central bank. Everybody knew it. The only uncertainty was whether

Thailand would default, which would ruin the speculators along with the Thai economy, or would devalue its currency.

It is easy to see where this was leading, because human cupidity and stupidity created opportunities. I've profited from these failings too; the Milwaukee Road yielded riches because the stigma of bankruptcy and the sorry history of railroads obscured a vast new opportunity. The unrealistic assessment of the future factored into the eurodollar calls reflected a typical human bias to project the future as a replay of the past, a failure to recognize when the game has changed. If Russia turns out to be as profitable as I think it will, it too will represent an opportunity resulting from investor vision clouded by the near past.

Most of my life I never thought of myself as rich. Indeed, only in the past few years have I been entirely free of debt. This may seem at first to be false modesty, but during the past five years, a number of very rich investors watched helplessly as their wealth disappeared. There was no reason to assume that I was immune to the quirks of fate that bring down the mighty.

A person who has a lot of money has few choices but to invest it or to give it away. As in my philosophy of investing, I tend to take a long view in philanthropy. In general, I prefer to give money to pursue a concept or idea. Among other things, I have given money to an archaeologist at Yale who is studying the impact of climate on the rise and fall of civilizations on the Habur Plain in what is now Syria. His findings, quite controversial in archaeological circles, suggest that severe drought, not civil war or invasion, brought about the end of the Akkadian civilization 4,200 years ago. I also currently sponsor an interdisciplinary program between the Rockefeller Institute and the Institute for Advanced Study to investigate the mathematical modeling of epidemics. People bring ideas to me, but quite often I think of a question I would like to have answered and then try to convince an institution to pursue that project.

A good deal of my philanthropy goes toward supporting archaeology and the arts. I fund the dig at Ashkelon in Israel because I'm interested in how different influences might surface as we unearth the past. The Roman arch we found that was built more than 1,000 years before Rome rose to power was precisely the kind of surprise we had been hoping for. The discovery underscored the sophistication of the Philistines. Lawrence Stager, the Harvard-based archaeologist in charge of the dig since its inception, argues that the Philistines were Mycenaean Greeks who established kingdoms on the eastern shores of the Mediterranean. Because we know many archaeologists, we also discovered one of the dirty secrets of the profession: archaeologists like to dig, but they don't always publish, and one reason is a lack of funding. So we started a fund for archaeological publication at Harvard University, and over the years we have funded scholars from around the world, many publishing reports on excavations that were concluded half a century ago.

I also believe that art history students should get out into the field to see the objects they are studying. To that end, I established a grant program at the Institute of Fine Arts in New York that gives graduate students who successfully complete the first year of study the funds to spend the summer anywhere in the world their studies might take them.

In philanthropy, as in business, I prefer to back a person rather than an institution. My aim in starting the Levy Economics Institute of Bard College was to support people and ideas. The ideas were my father's set of equations that predict the direction of profits and thus the course of an economy. The person was Leon Botstein, the president of Bard College, whom I first met in the 1970s. Leon is extraordinarily bright and far-sighted. The Levy Institute, housed in a beautiful Hudson River mansion, is a research institute where scholars gather to study the problems that first intrigued my father in 1912, with the goal of influencing business, labor, and government leaders to solve the pressing economic issues of our time.

When I first gave money to Bard, the college was very nearly broke, and it might have gone under had I not intervened. Now it is back on a better financial footing. Over the years, I have given or committed to Bard roughly $100 million. I'm willing to grant such a large sum because I believe liberal arts education is both important and imperiled. Even in the hypercompetitive world of Wall Street, most of the great names have been the products of a liberal arts education. The study of arts, ideas, history, and politics prepares students to enjoy life as well as contribute to society.

I give funds to institutions like Bard College with few strings attached. After all, what makes me think I'm smarter than the person running the institution? This makes me very popular because most people would rather give specific funds for a building that will be named after them, and donors who give money for the unglamorous chore of keeping a place going are few and far between. My reasoning, however, is nothing more than common sense: If you don't trust the people to whom you donate money to spend it wisely, you probably shouldn't be giving them money. The same goes for investing.

My involvement with some of the great minds in the sciences reveals the meagerness of my own achievements. Talk to a cosmologist at the Institute for Advanced Study, and any of our achievements on this puny planet shrinks to insignificance. All we can do is try to leave a legacy of good works.

If I had any doubts about my ephemeral successes, Philippe de Montebello, the director of New York's famed Metropolitan Museum of Art, put them into perspective. Philippe came to my home for breakfast one day to request our help in building a new Greek and Roman wing at the museum. He got somewhat carried away as he described the project, at one point offering to name the wing after Shelby and me in perpetuity.

Aware that sometime in the future Philippe's successor would probably be making the same promise to some donor not yet born, I asked him, "How long is 'in perpetuity'?" Without hesitating, he replied, "For you, fifty years." I laughed and thought about this for a moment, then suggested that we make it seventy-five since I guessed my daughter Tracy's feelings might be hurt if the name were changed during her lifetime. Philippe agreed, and the Metropolitan got its wing.

13

Honor Thy Father

THERE IS NO SYSTEM to beat the market. The future is never a simple replay of the past. In 2001 pundits constantly repeated the mantra that the market always rallies some six months after two successive interest rate cuts, but eleven rate cuts and a year later, the stock market has remained in the doldrums. The market has a life of its own, and a lifetime of investing has allowed me to develop instincts for the ways in which the markets and the economy affect each other.

In recent years, I have devoted much of my thought and my investment strategies to building on my father's work, focusing more on the direction the economy is likely to take than on individual stocks because the stock market is still overpriced. My predictions about the state of the economy will not come as a surprise to anyone who knows me. I have no crystal ball, but I believe we are in the early stages of a protracted recession and the value of the dollar will fall.

Any judgment about the future is a judgment about probabilities. In this case, I have given a high probability to my forecast of continuing recession and a falling dollar—say, two out of three chances. This might not seem a high probability, but the world is a complicated place, and two-thirds is significantly better than chance. I'm not alone in this prediction, of course; numerous articles have appeared in the press casting doubt on the strength of the recovery and expressing worry about the possibility of a double-dip recession. If I'm right, it will not be because I've identified correlations between events such as interest rate cuts and economic activity, but because the causal factors first described by my father have proved themselves once again.

This prediction derives directly from Dad's economics and from his understanding of the role corporate profits play in the economy. Even though the markets have changed greatly in recent years, the degree to which people save and the degree to which companies invest in capital goods still affect profits the way they did almost a hundred years ago. If debt burdens and concerns for the future cause the net savings rate to rise to its historical average of 6–10 percent, the country will be in deep trouble. Count on it. When the savings rate rises, my father observed, corporate profits fall. Today, each percentage point rise in the savings rate now decreases corporate profits by about $75 billion. This is not a correlation but a causal relationship that derives in some measure from the huge role that consumption plays in the U.S. economy. With total corporate profits amounting to about $680 billion a year ($860 billion at their peak during the boom years), a 1 percent increase in the savings rate would cut corporate profits by about 11 percent. (If corporate profits drop further, a 1 percent increase in the savings rate will carve an even bigger chunk out of earnings.) Currently, the savings rate is about 3 percent, not far above its recent lows. A rise by another 3 percent would knock about $225 billion from corporate profits, an enormous blow.

Smaller profits lead to less investment, which means fewer new jobs and more layoffs. Reduced earnings also depress stock prices, and with sky-high expectations still built into stock prices, investors could be in for a nasty shock. If conditions remain constant, the resumption of the recession might finally stall or reverse the rise in real estate prices, which could have severe repercussions on both the economy and consumer psychology because so much of the average family's wealth is tied up in the value of their home. The decline in the stock market will also affect the ability of pension funds to give people the retirement they had expected.

In the late 1990s, Americans went on a consumption binge, prompted in part by the illusion of wealth created by the stock market bubble and by ever-increasing real estate prices. Americans paid for this binge by taking on debt, paying for consumption with credit cards and home equity loans. Americans still have those debts, but they no longer can blithely assume that the markets will bail them out. Many workers will lose their jobs as employers try to cut expenses in the face of weak demand for their products. In all likelihood, consumer ebullience will gradually fade, and individuals will take a more realistic look at their financial situation. In the spring of 2002 only 21 percent of those polled by Moody's Investors Services expected incomes to be higher six months hence—a significant drop from the 25.7 percent average from 1996 to 2000. In the first quarter of 2002, real liquid assets dropped by an average of 24 percent per worker. As Americans' financial situation collides with reality, the savings rate will rise and profits will fall. Those who think we are in a recovery will be disappointed.

Only a dramatic increase in demand for American products, such as that seen during World War II, would cause businesses to build more capacity and build up their workforce. A pickup in demand would have the twofold impact of improving both business activity and the mood of the consumer.

Consumers may still be irrationally exuberant, but it's a safe bet they won't be perpetually irrationally exuberant. Indeed, they have been spending so much that there is little pent-up demand that might spur a surge in purchases. Moreover, all the major economies continue to struggle (Japan may be showing signs of life, but it is hardly a strong market for American products), and almost every industry has idle capacity. Thus, even if demand materialized, companies would have no pressing need for new capital spending. In January 2002 the government gave consumers an $80 billion tax break, enough to offset the hit on profits of about a 1 percent rise in savings. Tax breaks for businesses will improve corporate profits, and an increase in military spending will provide a shot in the arm for some industries.

But with the government running a deficit, it is unlikely that Congress will continue handing out tax breaks. Moreover, military spending can grow only so fast, and companies are not likely to build new factories unless they see a demand for their products over a period of time. We would need a huge stimulus package to offset the $225 billion drop that corporate profits would suffer if consumers resumed the savings habits they practiced for most of our history.

The savings rate is just one of a number of ingredients that affect profits. The negative balance of trade also casts a shadow on our future. For a long time, Americans have been buying far more oil and goods from other countries than they have been selling. With the exception of one minuscule blip in the early 1990s, the U.S. balance of trade has been negative since 1981. Until the mid–1990s, this did not adversely affect American lives, since the foreigners who sold us goods were perfectly happy to invest their dollars in America, keeping our accounts in balance even if we were buying more than we were selling abroad. Since then, however, foreigners have been taking out more than they have been reinvesting, and that process began accelerating toward the end of 2001.

The negative trade balance means that foreigners have been accumulating vast amounts of dollars. They hold these dollars by investing them in assets in the United States, by buying stocks, or by buying Treasury notes. Until 2001 they were rewarded for these investments in America because the dollar was continuously rising, giving those investors an added boost to their earnings from investments in real estate, stocks, bonds, and companies. Today these foreign holdings amount to about $2.2 trillion dollars, about 22 percent of the U.S. gross domestic product. That is a lot of dollars—enough to make these foreign holders a major player in the fate of our economy. In this respect, our well-being is determined by the mood of these foreign holders. Unfortunately, they seem to be getting a bit nervous as they evaluate the economy to which they have entrusted their wealth.

As recently as 2001, foreign investors saw budget surpluses extending throughout the coming decade (a good sign for those holding dollars), whereas they now see deficits resuming. No one is talking about paying off the national debt anymore, a silly idea anyway. These investors once saw the United States as the champion of free trade and accounting integrity, but they now see an administration imposing steel tariffs and a host of major companies rocked by accounting scandals. They also see private debt at astronomical levels and deteriorating corporate balance sheets.

Just out of view lurk even more frightening monsters. Overseas, low-wage economies such as China and India are gearing up to compete with the United States. Here at home, trillions of dollars of derivatives are held by virtually every major financial institution. We had a glimpse of the mischief that can sweep through the financial system when smart players like LTCM have bad luck with derivatives. If misfortune hits the giant government-supported finance corporations such as Fannie Mae or Freddie Mac, many large financial institutions in turn will suffer. These observations do not make the dollar holders less nervous.

Moreover, foreign holders of dollars are a sophisticated lot. They realize that U.S. politicians have to manage the economy in order to be reelected. They also know that elected leaders will even pitch ideology overboard to pander to constituents. The otherwise conservative Bush administration's decision to impose steel tariffs served as a timely reminder for those who might have forgotten this basic fact of American politics. Foreign investors also know that apart from tariffs, the biggest gift the government might give basic American businesses would be a weaker dollar, which would help boost their exports to other markets. While there will be a great temptation for the U.S. government to lower the value of the dollar, it will have little effect, because other countries will lower the value of their respective currencies.

By the spring of 2002, the dollar began to weaken. Since currencies tended to change direction less rapidly than other commodities, it was likely that the dollar would continue to decline and that other currencies would proportionately rise.

The weakening of the dollar would be driven more by the desire of nervous sellers to unload the currency than by any rush into an alternative. A host of alternatives to the dollar would probably rise, and they would rise in some respects independently of the normal factors that governed their movements. For instance, the yen might strengthen despite negative developments in Japan.

But where would the money go if people who held dollars sold them? The yen? The pound? The Swiss franc? The euro? Gold? It was a while before I took the euro seriously. From the moment of its announcement, I had been skeptical about its viability. I saw the euro as driven by an older generation of leaders in Europe who were preoccupied with the mayhem of the two world wars. Their reasonable concern with politics after two devastating wars caused them to obscure one obvious economic point: What would happen to the euro (or to the European Community, for that matter) when the prime minister of Italy or Spain was forced to tell his constituents that they had to live with massive unemployment during a recession because otherwise they would violate budget requirements imposed by German, French, and Belgian bureaucrats? All politics is local, after all, and I suspected that domestic political pressures would ultimately spell death for the euro. This may well happen in the long term, but in the meantime, the euro has emerged as a viable alternative to the dollar.

During the spring of 2002, I saw signs that the tides were shifting toward a declining dollar. The euro stopped falling relative to the dollar. As the euro stabilized and then began to rise, so did gold. (Gold has been the traditional refuge for investors in uncertain times, but the fall of 2001, the value of the precious metal had been steadily eroding since the 1980s.) The yen and the Swiss franc also started rising against the dollar. The yen rose despite the fact that ratings services were in the process of downgrading Japan's sovereign debt.

Time will tell if I am right about my judgment of the dollar and the euro. Indeed, I can be wrong more often than I am right, so long as the leverage on my correct judgments compensates for my mistakes. At least that is how my investments have worked out thus far. A statistician might deplore this approach, but it has worked for me for a half century.

For readers searching these pages for some secret formula for wealth, there is both good news and bad news. The bad news is that there is no secret formula that is concealed from all but a few powerful people with access to privileged information. The information that has guided my investments has almost always been public. If investors see successful financiers as akin to Sherlock Holmes—in the sense that they dig out recondite clues to the future of a stock or the markets—I'm more partial to the approach of Mycroft Holmes, who sat in his armchair and pondered the clues unearthed by his brother.

Success in finance remains an art rather than a science, if only because of the vagaries of human nature. Therein lies the good news: If investing is an art, it can be mastered. Practice is also important, as is the willingness to recognize your weaknesses and strive not to repeat the same mistake too often. If you want to follow a stock, the best way is to take a small position; practitioners always outperform professors. You must put yourself on the line.

My father, who felt that Wall Streeters were often overrewarded for activities that did not contribute to society's general well-being, disapproved of my career. Still, I believe he was also pleased that I chose to test his ideas in the marketplace and that his ideas have proved themselves time and again through the myriad challenges and changes of the past half century.

If I've had any advantage over other investors, it is that I had the benefit of growing up with Jerome Levy as a father. Dad did not view economics as a way to make money but as a way to improve society. Yet almost a century after he did his work, our problems continue. We have been through a period of deregulation, which has led to the excesses of the great bubble. The business community must remember that government has a role to play in our lives, whether it is through tax policy, regulation, or monitoring the rate of interest. We still have not figured out how to maintain full employment and a favorable balance of trade. Unless we can ameliorate these problems, our economic difficulties will continue. We will be prone to wide swings in the economy and in the stock market. And we may even have other bubbles to call our own.

Acknowledgments

If not for my wife, Shelby White, and her persistence and hard work, this book would not have been written.

My brother Jay is the heir to my father's work in economics. In large part, Jay's wisdom permeates these pages.

Wally Scheuer was my partner for many happy years. His father, Sy, taught me a lot by precept.

Jack Nash and I worked together for over half a century. Without Jack there would have been no Oppenheimer or very little of the financial ventures that are mentioned in these pages.

Archer Scherl, Jr. and I worked very closely at the founding of the Oppenheimer Funds. Without Archer's work the Funds would have been quite different and less successful than they became.

Ezra Merkin is one of the wisest men I met on Wall Street. He took the time from his busy schedule to read the manuscript. In a world divided by takers and givers, Ezra is a giver.

By profession Hadassah Brooks Morgan is a psychoanalyst, but really she's a philosopher who was very helpful to me. She is one of the wisest ladies I know.

Geraldine Fabrikant read a few pages when I first started writing the book and encouraged me to undertake the project. In fact, if she had not been so encouraging there might not have been a book.

Nancy Milford is a very dear friend. She spent countless hours going over the manuscript with me and exploring new approaches and directions the book should take.

Without my agent Esther Newberg there would not be a book.

My partner in this enterprise is Eugene Linden. Eugene is responsible for many of the clearest and most succinct parts of the book. Eugene is not only a dear friend but also a superb writer in his own right. He has written several books about apes and other animals, all of which made him particularly suitable to write a book about Wall Street.

Matthew Richards and Marc-Andre Pigeon were two fellows who came from the Levy Economics Institute of Bard College. Both of them worked diligently on research for the book. Their work was invaluable to me.

To my editor, Paul Golob, I hope he has easier clients to work with in the future. Paul should take the credit for having this book done in record time.

Peter Osnos, publisher of PublicAffairs, is a wonderful publisher. When the going got tough, as the saying goes, Peter was very tough. He has been outstanding, informed and helpful. I want to thank him and all of the staff at PublicAffairs.

Leon Botstein, president of Bard College and director of the American Symphony Orchestra, is one of the busiest and brightest men I have ever known. That he read the manuscript several times is a great act of friendship, which I will not forget.

I first met Eugene Rotberg many years ago at the SEC while

starting up the Oppenheimer Funds. At the time, I thought that he was one of the smartest people I met at the SEC. Nothing has changed my mind. Later on he became treasurer of the World Bank. He should be everybody's role model of a dedicated bureaucrat. He was kind to sit down with us and was of great help.

Alan Abelson, who wrote the foreword, was a high school and college chum of mine. Fifty years later I still love reading his column in *Barron's* on Saturday mornings. He is bright, witty, and unbiased. That's a wonderful combination.

Nina Berg runs my business organization, and without her I'd be lost.

I owe special thanks to my daughter Tracy and son-in-law, Lakshman, who discussed the book me on several occasions. Because of them, what might have been a chore turned out to be a joy.

Bob Lenzner is a special friend and magnificent journalist. His suggestions have been invaluable.

Thanks as well to Amanda Remus for her patient reading of the manuscript and for her thoughtful comments.

David Levy has carried the torch of Dad's economic work to the third generation. This work is becoming more and more important. I am pleased that fate has given me such a talented and gifted nephew.

Finally, Don Spiro did all the work at the Oppenheimer Management Co. Without Don there might not have been any Oppenheimer Management Fund.

Index

INDEX

INDEX

crash of 1987, 154–155
crash of 2002, 154–155
Crassus, 23
credit cards, 193
credit market
  shifts in, 149–150
  tightening during recessions, 183
Cuban missle crisis, 87
currencies
  devaluation of British pound,
    184–185
  devaluation of Thai baht, 186–187
  investment alternatives to U.S. dol-
    lar, 196–197

Davies, Edgar John, 79
De Angelis, Anthony, 158
dealmaking
  Heckler's preference for, 127
  segregating from other Oppen-
    heimer operations, 128
debt
  corporate, 159
  margin, 4
  peril of, 2
  recession and, 183
  savings and, 192–193
  U.S. public, 149, 194
Defense Mineral Exploration Admin-
    istration (DMEA), 82
deficit, U.S., 194
Delaney, Edmund, 80
demand, U.S. products, 193–194
depreciation, as tax incentive, 123
depression. *See* Great Depression
Der Aufbau, 49–50
deregulation
  excesses caused by, 199
  regulatory laxity and, 2–3
  regulatory standards, 4

derivatives
  hedge funds investing in, 138
  holdings of major financial institu-
    tions, 196
  market role in setting prices, 139
  psychological distortion of prices,
    143
Deuble, Albert, 48
disaggregation of conglomerates,
    132–136. *See also* leveraged buy-
    outs (LBOs)
  Odyssey Partners investing in, 132
  opportunities, 125
  TWC example, 132–135
disciplined investing, 105
distressed companies, 16. *See also*
    leveraged buyouts (LBOs)
dollar
  accumulation by foreigners,
    195–196
  devaluing, 196
  value of, 191–192
Donaldson, Lufkin, and Jenrette, 90
dotcoms, 160–161. *See also* Internet
Dow Jones Industrial Average
  highs of 2000, 1
  valuation of, 156
Dow 36,000 (Glassman and Hassett),
    156
Dreyfus Fund, 84
Dreyfus, Jack, 84–85
Dunbar, Nicholas, 143

earnings
  accountants manipulation of, 153
  ratio of Russian stock prices to, 179
  reports, 153
Eastern Gas and Fuel, 60–61
Economic Cycle Research Institute,
    167

208

INDEX

hi-tech stocks. *See also* Internet
flood of stock coincides with
decline in market, 160–161
market efficiency and, 147
Hidden Splendor Mines, 81–83
High-Risk Opportunities, 143
Hilary Minerals, 82
Hirsch and Company
author as research analyst for, 41,
45–48
decline of, 88, 91
Hirshman, Otto, 102–103
Histoire de l'Impôt (Ardant), 122
history, author's passion for, 22–23
home ownership, tax incentives,
123
hubris, LTCM incident and, 139
Hunt, Nelson Bunker, 53
Hunt, William Herbert, 53
Hutton, Ed, 75

I. G. Farben, 50
IBM typewriters, 106–107
Icahn, Carl, 135
India
low-wage economics of, 195
prospects of investing in, 178
inflation, 108
insider stock trades
attentiveness to, 54, 58
looking for patterns in, 33
watching Getty's moves, 55
Institute for Advanced Study, 142, 187,
189
Institute of Fine Arts, 188
interest, deducting interest paid on
mortgages, 123
interest rates
economic stimulation and, 182
eurodollar and, 181–183

as indicator of future prospects,
179–180
relating market rallies to, 191
Internet
belief that it would change world
economics, 156–157
fictional account of Internet stock
offering, 161–163
notion of risk and, 155–156
stock craze, 1
supermarket as analogy for understanding, 157
Interstate Commerce Commission
(ICC), 110
intuition, investing and, 177
Inventing Money (Dunbar), 143
inventory problems, new economy
and, 153
investment opportunities
badly managed companies, 106
bankruptcies and, 109, 111, 118
in China, 178
currency alternatives to U.S. dollar,
196–197
derivatives, 138
disaggregation, 132–136
government created, 186
in India, 178
junk bonds, 136, 142–143, 148–149
LBOs. *See* leveraged buyouts (LBOs)
municipal bonds, 125–126
mutual funds, 77
oil, 84
PUHCA related, 46
railroads, 58, 109–113
in Russia, 178–180, 183–184
S&Ls, 95–96
silver, 83
uranium, 82–83
investments. *See also* value investing
analysis and, 177

liquidation, (*cont.*)
  of LTCM, 144–145
Loeb, John L., 89–90
Long-Term Capital Management
  (LTCM), 137–149
  factors in collapse of, 138
  Federal Reserve's bailout, 146
  flaw in approach of, 142–143
  forced liquidation of, 144–145
  initial success of, 140–141
  lessons about market efficiency,
    147
  liquidation of hedge funds,
    143–144
  market undermines assumptions of,
    144
  principle players in, 138–139
  significance of, 150
  strategy of, 139–141
long-term perspective
  on investing, 55
  on markets, 23–24
low-wage economies, China and
  India, 195
Lowe, Richard, 83–84
Luchow's restaurant, 48
luck, financial success and, 16

Maastricht Treaty, 184
Madrick, Jeff, 157
management
  benefits of mutual funds to man-
    agement company, 127
  management contracts offered as
    part of LBOs, 126
  responsibility accompanying LBOs,
    127
  shareholder interest contrasted with
    interest of, 134
margin debt, 4

margin, profit margins during 1990s,
  152
margin requirements, 43
market crashes
  money supply shrinking with, 10–11
  Soros attack on pound and, 184
market research, 85
market share, Internet business focus
  on, 156
markets. *See also* "efficient market"
  1990s, 20, 156
  accounting and regulatory stan-
    dards and, 4
  adjusting to changes in, 9
  bear markets, 168
  bond analysts and, 160
  bubbles, 151
  bull markets, 13, 166, 168
  factors in changes, 20–21
  generational memory and, 8
  irrationality of, 9
  liquidation of hedge funds and, 144
  long-term perspective, 23–24
  LTCM and, 142
  meltdowns, 184
  no system for beating, 191
  odds against cashing out at top, 10
  psychology of, 1, 8–10, 21
  "reversion to mean," 168
  timeliness of, 184
  unpredictability of, 12
  unwarranted optimism in current,
    172
  value basis of, 13
Martin, Preston, 96–97
Mass Mutual, 132–136
McGinnis, Patrick B., 34
McKinsey and Company, 152
McMillen, Thomas R., 117
media, maelstrom of, 21
Mercantile House, 130–131

Index

Meriwether, John, 138, 141
Merton, Richard, 138, 141
Metropolitan Museum of Art, 189–190
Meyer, André, 118
The Mikado, 147
military spending, 194
Milken, Michael, 3, 99, 136
Mills, Wilbur, 124
Milwaukee Road. *See* Chicago, Milwaukee, St. Paul & Pacific Railroad
Minsky, Hyman, 35
Mission Corporation, 56–57
money
   as prerequisite of freedom, 39
   supply shrinks with market crashes, 10–11
Montebello, Philippe de, 189–190
Montgomery Ward, 44
Morris, Willie, 101
mortgages
   adjustable-rate, 96–98
   deducting interest paid on, 123
   "mortgaging out," 125
municipal bonds, 125–126
mutual funds
   benefits to management company, 78
   fees based on performance, 79–80
   investing profits from LBOs in, 125
   offshore, 99
   oil investment as, 84
   Oppenheimer and Co. movement into, 77–78
   strategies, 78

Nasdaq
   evaporation of wealth, 153
   highs of 2000, 1
   losses of 2001, 10, 152

Nash, Jack
   on capital shortages during bad times, 91
   leadership of, 89
   management of LBOs, 127
   Milwaukee Road deal and, 116
   partnership with, 17
   reorganization of Oppenheimer and Co., 128–129
   role in Odyssey Partners, 131
   role in Oppenheimer and Co., 65–66
National Scholarship Fund and Service for Negro Students, 73
nationalism, 38–39
new economy
   illusions of, 6–7
   inventory problems and, 153
   productivity gains and, 152–153
New York City, taxes on unincorporated businesses, 121–122
The New York Review of Books, 157
The New York Times
   on dangers of accounting laxity, 3–4
   on Enron accounting, 158, 164
   on performance of Oppenheimer Fund, 86
   on sale of Oppenheimer, 130
   story about Jerome Levy in, 27
   TWC ad campaign in, 134
Newman, Mickey, 51
Nixon, President Richard, 5, 101
Nobel Prize, 138, 146
nonrecourse money, borrowing, 126–127
Norfolk and Western railroad, 61
Norris, Floyd, 4, 164
nuclear energy, 83

Odlum, Floyd, 82–83
Odyssey Partners, 131–132
offshore funds, 99
Ogilvie, Richard, 114, 116
Ohio River Company, 59–60
"old boy network," 42
Olivetti, 106
Oppenheimer and Co.
  author's role as partner in, 15, 48–49
  colleagues at, 65–66
  founding, 48
  investing outside the stock market in the 60s and 70s, 108
  Jewish/non-Jewish partners, 88
  Milwaukee Road and, 115, 116
  mutual funds investments, 77–78
  non-typical nature of, 49
  oil investments, 83–84
  opening new offices of, 50
  projections by money managers, 9–10
  reorganization of, 129
  sale of, 129–131
  salesmanship test used by, 87–88
  silver investments, 83
Oppenheimer, Ernest, 106
Oppenheimer Fund
  Buehl and, 99
  founding, 15
  as hedge fund, 80–81
  performance record of, 86–87
  purchase of Underwood stock by, 106
  reaction to launch of, 79
  selecting symbol for, 85–86
  uranium investment by, 82–83
Oppenheimer Funds
  auctioned to Mass Mutual, 131
  directors of, 18
  founding, 79
  rapid growth of, 128

Oppenheimer, Max
  dominant role in Oppenheimer and Co., 65
  trading in sperrmarks, 47–48
opportunities. *See also* investment opportunities
  badly managed companies as, 106
  identifying unexploited, 16
  relationship to risk, 94
  undervalued stocks and, 168
order, 11
outside interests, 74
overreachers
  accounting scandals and, 93–94
  Cornfield example, 98–99
  Fenton example, 94–98
  King (John) example, 100–101
  Zeckendorf example, 102–104

Pacific Western Oil Company, 56
Paribas, 133
partnership structure
  advantages of to Oppenheimer and Co., 89–90
  liabilities associated with, 128
Pei, I. M., 102
perspective
  long-term, 23–24, 55
  viewing present from perspective of past, 18
philanthropy, 187–190
  author's involvement with, 74–75
  backing people rather than institutions, 189–190
  supporting archaeology and arts, 188–189
  tax incentives supporting, 123
Philistines, 22
The Picture of Dorian Gray, 163
Pierce, Dan, 46

PublicAffairs is a publishing house founded in 1997. It is a tribute to the standards, values, and flair of three persons who have served as mentors to countless reporters, writers, editors, and book people of all kinds, including me.

I. F. STONE, proprietor of *I. F. Stone's Weekly*, combined a commitment to the First Amendment with entrepreneurial zeal and reporting skill and became one of the great independent journalists in American history. At the age of eighty, Izzy published *The Trial of Socrates*, which was a national bestseller. He wrote the book after he taught himself ancient Greek.

BENJAMIN C. BRADLEE was for nearly thirty years the charismatic editorial leader of *The Washington Post*. It was Ben who gave the *Post* the range and courage to pursue such historic issues as Watergate. He supported his reporters with a tenacity that made them fearless and it is no accident that so many became authors of influential, best-selling books.

ROBERT L. BERNSTEIN, the chief executive of Random House for more than a quarter century, guided one of the nation's premier publishing houses. Bob was personally responsible for many books of political dissent and argument that challenged tyranny around the globe. He is also the founder and longtime chair of Human Rights Watch, one of the most respected human rights organizations in the world.

For fifty years, the banner of Public Affairs Press was carried by its owner, Morris B. Schnapper, who published Gandhi, Nasser, Toynbee, Truman, and about 1,500 other authors. In 1983, Schnapper was described by *The Washington Post* as "a redoubtable gadfly." His legacy will endure in the books to come.

Peter Osnos, *Publisher*